Australia's Introduced Animals and Plants

Gary Twyford

REED

Acknowledgements

Gathering material for this book could not have been done without the considerable help and advice of a great many people.

Considerable assistance with research material was obtained from the staff and facilities of the Latrobe Reference Library, Melbourne, the Keith Turnbull Research Centre, Victoria, the Vermin and Noxious Weeds Board, Victoria, the Department of Primary Industry Library and the Burnley Horticultural College, Victoria.

I am also indebted to Mrs Hilary Campbell who typed the original manuscript.

A special thank you to Hugh Sherrit and his wife Sue for their encouragement and for sharing their love of the outdoors. And finally, thank you to my wonderful wife, Kerri, and son, Blair, who supported and encouraged me in every way; and for their untiring patience in waiting for me on countless occasions whilst I slipped into the bush with my well-worn excuse: 'I just want to get a photograph of something.'

First published 1991 by
Reed Books Pty Ltd
3/470 Sydney Rd, Balgowlah NSW 2093

© Text and Photography Gary Twyford

All rights reserved. No part of this publication may be reproduced, stored in a retrieval system, or transmitted in any form or by any means, electronic, mechanical, photocopying, recording or otherwise, without the prior written permission of the publishers.

National Library of Australia
Cataloguing-in-Publication data

Twyford, Gary A. (Gary Alan), 1946–
Introduced animals and plants of Australia.

Includes index.
ISBN 0 7301 0361 7.

1. Animal introduction – Australia. 2. Plant introduction – Australia. I. Title.

574.50994

Typeset in Australia by Solo Typesetters, S.A.
Printed in Singapore by Times Offset

CONTENTS

INTRODUCTION / 4

EFFECTS OF INTRODUCED ANIMALS AND PLANTS / 6

WILD ANIMALS / 11

Red Deer / 11
Fallow Deer / 12
Sambar Deer / 14
Hog Deer / 15
Rusa Deer / 16
Chital Deer / 33
Blackbuck Antelope / 34
Fox / 35
Rabbit / 37
European Hare / 40
Cane Toad / 41
Rats and Mice / 43

FERAL ANIMALS / 45

Brumby / 46
Donkey / 47
Camel / 48
Water Buffalo / 65
Other Wild Cattle / 66
Wild Pig / 67
Wild Goat / 68
Feral Cat / 70
Feral Dog / 71
Dingo / 73

BIRDS / 77

House Sparrow / 78
Hedge Sparrow / 79
Starling / 79
Blackbird / 80
Song Thrush / 81
English Skylark / 82
Indian Mynah / 83
European Goldfinch / 84
European Greenfinch / 85
Red-whiskered Bulbul / 85
Mute or White Swan / 85
Indian Spotted and Senegal Turtle
    Dove / 86
Indian Peafowl / 87
Cattle Egret / 88
Ringneck Pheasant / 88
Chukar Partridge and California
    Quail / 89
Mallard Duck / 90
Feral Pigeon / 91
Ostrich / 92
Feral Turkey / 93
Feral Domestic Fowl / 93

FISH / 94

Brown Trout / 95
Rainbow Trout / 96
Eastern Brook Trout / 97
Atlantic Salmon / 97
Quinnat Salmon / 98
European Perch or Redfin / 98
Coarse Fish: Tench, Roach and
    Dace / 99
Carp / 101
Goldfish / 102
Aquarium Fish / 102
Mosquito Fish or Gambusia / 103
Pacific Oyster / 103

INSECTS / 104

PLANTS / 113

Summary of Introductions / 124

Index / 127

INTRODUCTION

Australia today is often called the 'Lucky Country'; its inhabitants enjoy one of the highest standards of living in the world. We are great rural producers and exporters, with virtual seas of grain; sheep and cattle numbering many millions; fruits and vegetables of every kind are now grown in abundance, and the land is rich in minerals.

However, our present state of prosperity was certainly not anticipated by the early explorers. The opinion of the English navigator Captain William Dampier, on landing on the West Australian coast in 1688, reads in part:

The land is of a dry soil, destitute of water
The woods are not thick, nor the trees very big.
There was plenty of long grass growing under the trees, but it was very thin.
We saw no trees that bore fruits or berries.
We saw no sight of Animal nor any tracks of beast, but once; of a wild dog.
Neither sheep, poultry or fruits of the earth are in evidence.

Even after Captain James Cook's discovery of the east coast in 1770, and Captain Phillip's landing in New South Wales in 1788, all things necessary to support and sustain the Europeans' lives had to be brought with them.

This new land had no animals, birds and plants such as those found in Europe, which the new settlers could round up, domesticate or fence in. Since settlement only one native edible plant, the macadamia nut, has found sufficient acceptance to be grown in commercial quantities.

Meat could be had from kangaroos, but they were wild and flighty. There were no birds that could be quickly tamed so that their eggs could be gathered regularly. Of vegetables and fruits there were few that were plentiful, and fewer still that tasted anything like those grown in Europe. It was frighteningly obvious that Europeans would have to live as the native Aborigines did just to survive in Australia, if it were not for the food ships with their precious cargoes from England.

From the beginning, it was important that attempts be made to ensure that the penal colony was at least self-sufficient in food stuffs. It was unwise to rely on ships from abroad, whose lengthy voyages were fraught with difficulties and dangers. It was quickly noticed that most things could be grown well; livestock seemed to thrive, and there was an abundance of good grazing land.

The population grew steadily but when gold, and vast amounts of it, was discovered in Victoria not long after John Batman's founding of Melbourne, the scramble was on. People came from all over the world to swell the population, so that it doubled its size in a year. Apart from those that flocked to the diggings, eager free settlers arrived by the score, hoping for new opportunities and a new life.

Instant wealth was made not only from the gold itself, but by supplying all manner of equipment, clothing, foodstuffs, timber and other provisions to the prospectors. Settlers and merchants very often made more money than the diggers themselves.

Everything seemed to be in short supply and much in demand. More sheep and cattle were imported and raised; in fact, all domestic animals were urgently required. More fruit trees were planted and all manner of crops were sown.

Great wealth came to many in this short

explosive period, so that Australia developed from a seeming wilderness to a society modelled on that of England.

Now the prospectors set about constructing large and fine houses with splendid gardens in traditional English styles. Imposing public buildings sprang up, and theatre societies and drama clubs were formed. Those involved in constructing this new society were homesick for the United Kingdom; Australia seemed such a harsh country in both climate and terrain. The bush seemed drab compared to the gentle green countryside of Britain.

In Australia, the new settlers established their houses, buildings and societies as they had at home. They had their vegetables, crops, fruits and livestock about them. If there was anything they were missing it was decorative plants and the wildlife of Britain. They were so determined in their re-creation, that they transported England's customs, and traditions too.

They cast a critical eye on the native landscape. It was not that there were no animals to hunt, birds to hear or fish to catch. It was that they were so foreign, so different. So unusual were they that the likes of them had not been seen or heard of anywhere else in the world. What this country needed, it was decided, were the song birds of England, the deer and other animals worthy of the hunt, and more familiar creatures that were so appealing to the European eye.

Some wild animals and other creatures were imported and released from the earliest days of settlement but in 1857 the Victorian Zoological Society was formed. It was followed in 1860 by the Acclimatization Society. These bodies organised the importation of plants, animals, birds, fish and other creatures with the express purpose of setting them free in the wild. In the societies' opinion this could only be beneficial to the new country.

Creatures and plants were brought to Australia to satisfy one of three main purposes (or a combination of them). The deer, rabbit, fox, trout and many others were brought for sport; many varieties of birds and plants were brought for ornamental purposes; and there were those species such as the alpacas and angora goats that might prove to be of economic value for their meat, skin or wool.

Most introductions were from the settlers' homeland of England, for these were the creatures they knew best. Many other creatures were known to the English from areas in the far flung colonies of their Empire. Giant snakes from Africa were considered and birds that kill snakes; monkeys were tried. In fact, anything that crawled, walked, slithered, flew or swam, was considered for possible introduction to Australia.

Many of the ludicrous and outright dangerous suggestions of possible imports were not made by ordinary folk; it was the much respected and learned 'pillars of society', which planned this virtual 'Noah's Ark'. These very same citizens were, in most cases, responsible for bringing in the creatures that proved later to be the most troublesome.

The new arrivals were to be kept and acclimatised in Royal Park, Melbourne. Ironically, it was the park from which Burke and Wills embarked on their incredible journey, overland to the Gulf of Carpentaria in 1860. So as the new animal arrivals were landing, explorers were setting off to discover what was already here; the land, its creatures, plants, and birds.

The societies had virtually no knowledge of the country. For all they knew Australia could have contained any one of the creatures and plants that were going to great trouble and expense to bring in. What happened and why, is an important part of our history. The consequences of wrong decisions and mistakes (and there were many) are still with us.

So great has the influence of introductions been, that today most of us do not live in a truly Australian environment but rather a created European one. All of the development and change that has taken place with settlement has caused the native creatures and plants to give way, to retreat, and we have replaced many with introduced species. The flowers and plants of our gardens, the grasses of our lawns, the trees of our parks, mostly came from overseas. Our food animals, our fruits, grains and vegetables, familiar birds, and the creatures of our towns and cities originated in other lands.

What can be learnt of this exotica, of this new wildlife that now lives amongst us? Some were deliberately set free; others came in unnoticed, their introduction was accidental. Others simply escaped captivity or were abandoned, How and where do they all live in Australia today?

Effects of Introduced Animals & Plants

Australia's new wildlife, both of deliberate and accidental introduction, has had considerable impact on this country. Some have been classed as desirable and even beneficial. Many others are declared pests or vermin; the rabbit, fox, feral cat and cane toad are obviously deserving of their pest status. Many introductions are considered almost entirely in terms of economic cost: the loss and reduction in yield they cause in agricultural production.

Detrimental effects on native flora and fauna, either from direct or indirect competition for food and habitat, predation etc, or by becoming victims of controls implemented against other pests, are usually only secondary considerations.

The effects of introductions, then, are generally evaluated from a particular perspective, and of course, the evaluation is dependent on the criteria used in the judgement. For example, a simplistic and purist view could be taken resulting in the stand that all introductions are bad because for every mouthful of food an introduced creature takes, it does so at the direct expense of a native. Similarly, it could be said that each introduced plant takes up space that might be better occupied by a native.

Rather than sing the praises of those responsible for importing what may be considered desirable or beneficial and to decry and apportion blame to those responsible for the importing of disasters, or attempt to itemise what effect each individual wild introduction may have had, effort should be spent gaining an appreciation of the overall influences, circumstances and consequences which were involved in bringing about the long-term effects.

This necessarily involves looking closely at the history of Australia. Australia as a continent is relatively isolated and very old geologically. It developed along a different evolutionary path to other land masses. It is the driest continent on earth; it has extremes of temperature and unreliable seasons; it fluctuates between times of plenty and periods of drought. Such factors have caused the evolution of unique flora and fauna.

The original human inhabitants, nomadic Aboriginals, were hunter gatherers. They did not cultivate crops nor build permanent shelters. They did not have any domesticated animals to provide reliable and convenient sources of food. Theirs was a culture which remained relatively unchanged for thousands of years. They were at one with nature, rather than attempting to bend the land to their will, as European man had done.

The first European settlers were from Britain, a gentle land, tamed by civilisation; a country of order, conformity, even regimentation, with management and control pervading.

The rural areas consisted of closely settled small farms, which were both well organised and highly productive. Creatures such as the fox and rabbit were always kept well in check by abundant cheap labour and good farm management. This limited breeding areas and cover for wild animals and their populations thus were controlled.

The settlers were not interested in accepting this land for what it was. It could scarcely have been more different from what they were used to, so they set about trying to make it more familiar.

Scrub was cleared to open up country for grazing. Sheep and cattle were rapidly increasing in numbers everywhere, and as soon as the native grasses were eaten down in one area, they moved on to new ones.

Never, in their previous long history, had the grasses, plants and shrubs been subjected to this type of grazing. Much of the indigenous flora could not cope. Plants did not have the time to flower and seed, nor did they have the time to evolve mechanisms to ensure their survival from this onslaught.

Many were ill-equipped to restore themselves after the sharp cloven hooves of the exotic animals trampled them and cut into them, moved soil and shifted stones that had held them in shallow and fragile soils. For countless centuries these plants had only been subjected to the soft padded feet of native grazers and there were far fewer of them.

The virgin forests held massive trees that were being felled for the very first time and not cut down in ones and twos, but in their thousands.

Strong light and drying winds gained entry to ground that had previously been sheltered, so that the levels of humidity and temperature were altered; mosses, fungi, lichen, the understorey plants and the creatures that lived amongst them had to try to cope with something new. Where could they go? Most of the forests now were similarly affected and not in small patches that normally would have been the case when the odd forest giant toppled over after it reached maturity. Heavy rain could now strike the ground hard, in big droplets, whereas when the forest was in its natural state, the overhead canopy of leaves normally reduced its velocity to something like a gentle mist. Understorey plants and the forest creatures had evolved to accept only this.

The grazing and clearing of vegetation in open country, and in forests, allowed the combination of heavy rain, wind and direct sunlight to have a huge impact on the ground surface. Plants and their roots, now so exposed, could no longer hold the soil together which caused the soil and its nutriment-rich mulch of leaves and other debris to be washed and blown away. The ground became eroded and rivers became silted up, altering their natural flow rate, course and temperature, which affected whatever lived in them or depended on them. Waterways were further altered by increased human and animal use of them, and by dams and other constructions.

Locusts enjoyed the newly-opened countryside. They were to be seen in swarms of millions, sometimes reported to even block out the sun. They travel great distances and have been tracked by radar to cover distances of six hundred kilometres overnight. Their voracious appetite is frightening; one property owner had forty acres of a one metre high crop reduced to bare earth in no more time than it took him to telephone nine of his neighbours to warn them of the impending onslaught. It is said that locusts will eat anything green, and stories tell of them eating green clothes hanging on a washing line so completely that only the buttons remained on the ground. A story is also told of an outback house that was painted green and had all its paint eaten. The lead contained in the paint caused the locusts to die of lead poisoning, and the resulting stench from the millions of rotting bodies caused the family to vacate the house.

Creatures as small as native stickfast fleas that had previously only lived on kangaroos, possums, wombats and snakes, now adapted to live on the fox, the introduced rats and mice, and especially the rabbit.

The native heliothus moth ate so much of the cotton that was grown, and increased its numbers so much as a result, that it has prevented this crop from being grown in some areas. Even microscopic parasites, with all of their complicated life cycles, learned to live in new hosts.

Originally diverse communities of plants and creatures (where few of each type were normally present) were changed to almost single species environments or monocultures of dense concentrations.

This of course was deliberately done in agriculture to achieve higher production of desirable plants but always with it came a higher proportion of the undesirables, in the form of living things that could take advantage of the new conditions.

Control of many creatures and plants, both introduced and native, became absolutely necessary as their populations exploded. Poisoning was how it was mainly achieved.

Many used poisons like some people take medicine—if the prescription calls for one teaspoon two must do you twice as good.

If it was seen to kill scores of birds and other innocents it was considered to be a measure of its potency. It was only later, after poison was spread in enormous quantities over huge areas of land, that its specificity to the particular pest in question could be gauged—so many innocents suffered.

Many people worked as poisoners for a living; it was their trade.

DDT was a simple and convenient name, but its real name is 'Dichlorodiphenyl trichloroethane'—it was too much to expect ordinary folk to learn to say it, or spell it, let alone understand from what it is made, how it worked, and on what and why.

The poisons became so widespread that many creatures died outright. Some accumulated poisons in their bodies so that when others ate them they died or their young died. Some young birds were enclosed in shells too brittle and weak to see them through till hatching. Such were the consequences of indiscriminate use.

But then, *everything* was a pest to the majority of those who sought an income from the land. Bandicoots, bustards and bilbies; wombats, warrigals and wedge-tailed eagles; kangaroos and koalas—they were all controlled in some way.

The plants sheep and cattle found palatable became less common; the unpalatable ones, more common. And so it was with the prey of predators.

The natural stable and unmodified plant communities of high density and diversity had these physical barriers to invasion broken, which allowed the strong competitive weeds to gain available space and successfully compete for the essentials required for growth.

Change had occurred quickly on a massive scale. It was a gross transformation and a dramatic, turbulent upheaval of what had been the natural state for so long. What had occurred to native creatures had not been done deliberately; it was not a planned, callous attempt to upset the balance of what had been; it was simply a consequence.

Presumably little account or consideration was given to any of the requirements of the native flora and fauna.

Birds' beaks are designed in length and shape according to their food preference. The native honeyeaters evolved to obtain nectar and pollinate many of the unusual plants here since we were without large honey bees. Different species of these birds may all feed off the same flower, for each has a different length of beak and reaches into the flower to a different depth. The large and colourful parrots and cockatoos have massive strong beaks, and the means to hold the large seeds produced by many native shrubs and trees. However nature has ensured that some seeds fall from their imperfect grasp to germinate the next generation of shrubs and trees and, in turn, the birds' future food requirements.

The small pretty finches of the desert have beaks that cope with the strange plants that grow there and help disperse them wherever they fly. The plants are equally dependent and adapted to such birds.

Change was to overtake them all. Some creatures still had their shelter, but not their particular food source; others had food, but no suitable shelter and sadly, some had neither. The native creatures and plants that could not accept these changes were forced to vacate their range, to move on or perish; unfortunately, some did perish.

On the other hand, some native creatures and plant species took advantage of the changes that had taken place, for change had improved their lot. White cockatoos, galahs, cockateils, corellas, and a host of other seed-eaters began to take advantage of the new seed as quickly as it was spread upon the ground or when the seed heads of crops ripened.

Insects and grubs of all kinds busied themselves in what the settlers planted. Native rats and mice did too. Native birds that ate insects, rats and mice now had a larger food source and so their numbers increased. Snakes and goannas also grew fat on these new populations.

More grazing lands with conveniently placed waterholes were a boon to native grazing animals, such as kangaroos and wallabies. They quickly multiplied as a result.

In all booming populations, there are those that are weak and sick, dead and dying, on which others may prey. The native hawks, eagles, harriers and kites, owls, crows, native cats and dingoes, amongst others, all took advantage of this feast and bred more of their kind.

One attitude seems to have been, 'If they don't eat the grass or crops, perhaps money could be made from their skins or meat'.

Fences now crossed areas where emus had migrated for countless centuries; there was a bounty paid on presentation of their beaks, and they weren't the only creatures with a bounty on their heads. Perhaps some of it can be excused, for the settlers endured incredible hardship and suffering to break in this, the harshest of lands.

The majority of pests must be tolerated and controlled, for on balance, they are the disadvantages weighed against the advantages won; a cost incurred in obtaining such abundant production.

Ongoing controls will be required and the challenge is to find better and more effective ones. Almost certainly this will include bringing in more exotics, in the form of natural or biological controls.

Commercial harvesting to control or reduce pest species has never worked, simply because as long as the pest has some commercial value, sufficient quantities of it will always remain. This is the case with the fox, feral pig and kangaroos.

Commercial harvesting initially reduces the population; however, it soon stabilises (given seasonal fluctuations) to the point where the commercial harvest merely keeps pace with breeding capacity. Often those responsible for a pest's control have a vested interest in a viable population.

As pest species are generally prolific breeders, they seem to fill available niches with apparent disregard to culling. Static figures, over many years, of both the seasonal take and the populations of those that remain attest to that.

Of the species we wish to retain, such as kangaroos, albeit in reduced numbers, use of species-specific hormonal breeding suppressants might be investigated. In America, they have had some success in reducing the breeding capacity of the fully protected mustangs or wild horses which were beginning to seriously overpopulate their designated range.

The continuous threat to Australia of the introduction of serious exotic diseases may mean that consideration should be given to the elimination, by induced controlled disease epidemics, of animals that might act as carriers, for example foxes, feral pigs and feral cats.

Consideration could also be given, prior to such control action, to the concept of confined raising of commercially valuable species, such as the fox, if skins are required, as currently occurs with sable and mink in many overseas countries.

The concept of artificial rearing of threatened native species is worthy of further investigation and application; this concept has worked continuously and remarkably well here with the introduced trout. In recent years, some native species of fish, crocodiles, giant clams and prawns have been raised in hatcheries for commercial gain, with a designated proportion of production being made available for release back to the wild. Much valuable research and understanding is gained from such operations, which are self-funding, due to the commercial value of the product and the spin-off of the growing tourist industry.

Artificial rearing could be advantageously extended here to include native butterflies, birds and flowers. Some countries are already involved in such programmes, where they have found, in addition to the benefits already mentioned, that the pressure on wild populations is reduced, due to the availability of collectible specimens to bona-fide collectors. This undermines the illegal trafficking and smuggling of such species.

We must begin to deal effectively with the problems of land degradation, erosion and salinity, and to see the advantages to our landscape and wildlife re-afforestation and habitat restoration programmes.

It may even become compulsory in future for private land of a certain size to have a designated area for native flora in which native creatures may find sanctuary and one day approach their original distribution.

It goes without saying that had some control, however minor, been in place long ago, we would not have problems of the magnitude we face today.

Our future is about restoration, management and control of what we already have, and keeping out what we do not need or want.

Our quarantine and customs services rigorously search for accidental introductions. They must continue to do this. Each year they confiscate tonnes of foreign prohibited material which could threaten the wellbeing of this country and its wildlife.

The authorities are all but overwhelmed by the increasing numbers of travellers and tourists who expose us to serious risks by accidentally or deliberately introducing illegal exotica. They try to bring in such things as cheeses, fruits, meats and plants, seeds in pockets, tortoises in suitcases, and fish in plastic bags.

One suspicious looking traveller with a decided limp was found to have a plum seedling a metre long, with an accompanying root ball in soil, stuffed down the leg of his trousers. Whatever variety of plum it was, we are sure to have it here already, for we export the fruit and disease free root-stocks of every variety.

There is a need for continuing education of the general public. This may assist the quarantine and customs authorities in their role. Should travellers and others become better informed of the variety of goods available here there would be no need for them to try to bring in their own.

Many travellers, for one reason or another, fail to comply with the requirement to declare 'risk goods'. They might be better encouraged to declare them if there was a system whereby they received a voucher in exchange for what they voluntarily handed in. It could be done on a like-for-like basis whereby the goods were procurable at reduced cost or free from a producer here on presentation of the voucher.

The serious risks we face may require novel approaches for we cannot expect to always apprehend all contraband.

It is most unlikely that there will be any further deliberate introductions of exotic wild animals, birds or fish. However, this is not to say that there are not those who enthusiastically propose such introductions.

A recent example of such a proposal concerned a quick-growing grass from South America. It was hailed as having enormous potential for the cattle industry of northern Australia.

It was enthusiastically proposed that if the Ord River Valley was planted with this grass, more cattle could be produced there than in the Kimberleys and the whole of the Northern Territory combined. When thoroughly investigated here, it was found that the grass makes the hair of cattle fall out and affects the function of their thyroid gland; this does not occur in cattle where the grasses originate.

The Nile perch, a large fish of sporting potential from Africa, was the most recent wild creature considered for release here. Following the proposal, research showed that the Nile perch could decimate native fish populations in waters where it was released or colonised through accident.

Australia is unique when compared to other countries in that the consequences of European settlement have had a disproportionately adverse effect on native plants and creatures. An important contributing factor was the mass introduction here of domestic and wild creatures and plants. However, there are encouraging signs that valuable lessons have been learned and that a new enlightened attitude will be applied in the future to animals, birds, plants and fish, where the emphasis will be to make better use of natives.

WILD ANIMALS

Red Deer

When it was decided to bring wild animals to Australia, the various species of deer would probably have been one of the first to be considered. For deer in general, and the red deer in particular, represent everything that a wild animal should be. They are appreciated for their grace, beauty and timid nature, yet in the mating season represent nature's law of 'the survival of the fittest' more obviously than do most other species. The stags roar, bellow and charge with clashing antlers, to prove in physical battle who is the strongest to breed the next generation.

Most early settlers, coming from Europe, were quite used to seeing deer in the forests, parks and woodlands of their homeland. So from the 1880s onwards, the acclimatisation societies and some private individuals brought in deer from many regions of the world. Some fifteen or so different species were introduced, however only six species exist in the wild of Australia today.

It was hoped that the deer's presence here would not only remind settlers of home, but would also provide a variety of large game animals worthy of the hunt and would provide tasty meat, of which there seemed a general absence in this country. The settlers found our large native animals, the kangaroos and emus, lacked sporting qualities and tasted too strange to be palatable. The native creatures merely sat or stood, innocent and inquisitive, at the approach of the new white man, mounted on a horse and armed with a stick that made a noise and fired hot lead.

The red deer are majestic, impressive animals and were the prize game of

hunters. They are a large deer, reddish tan in colour, weighing about 150 kg and standing over a metre at the shoulder. They have a magnificent set of antlers reaching another metre above their head. Little wonder they have figured so much in stories, poetry and paintings.

The red deer has proved so popular that it has spread from its native regions of northern Africa, Europe and the Middle East to nearly every country in the world, including New Zealand, Argentina, Chile, the USA, and Australia. Although this deer was introduced to most states here, they failed to establish themselves in many areas. However, today we have them in Queensland and New South Wales in good numbers, and somewhat smaller herds in Victoria and Western Australia.

It is strange that they have not colonised more areas, as they are great wanderers, more so than most other deer, often covering fifteen to thirty kilometres during the day and night whilst feeding. The red deer's ability to walk vast distances is legendary, and whilst they are content to graze the high country of New South Wales during the summer months, with the onset of the winter snows they migrate the many kilometres necessary to take them to the milder climate over the border in Victoria. As the snow recedes they return once more to their former range. It must be that this area of Victoria does not offer them what they require all year round, or they would be more likely to stay there permanently.

Red Deer

In all areas where red deer can be found, their numbers appear to be rather static. This indicates that here in Australia they have reached the numbers that their habitat can support, although in other countries to which they have been introduced they have spread alarmingly, often necessitating control.

Red deer prefer an open habitat, particularly in summer, and it is during this time that the pretty red and white spotted calves can be seen. Born during November and December, what a wonder they are. They are capable of finding their mother's milk only fifteen minutes after their birth, and they can walk, although a little unsteadily, only forty-five minutes after entering the world. This is nature's way of affording them some chance against predators.

It is also throughout the hot weather that the muddy pools of the deer wallows can be discovered along the shoreline of lakes and the banks of rivers and streams, which are abundant throughout their range. The deer create these large depressions in the soft ground at the water's edge by pawing away with the front feet, allowing water to seep in, until the pool is large enough for them to sit and roll in. They wallow frequently as it helps their skin and coat, and rids them of annoying insects. Perhaps they also do it for the sheer enjoyment of the cooling effects on a hot day.

The red deer has not become a problem in Australia. In fact, this proud and majestic animal doesn't look out of place in our mountain ranges. It always elicits admiration from those fortunate enough to encounter it in the wild.

Fallow Deer

Of the six varieties of deer remaining in Australia today, the fallow are by far the most numerous and widespread. They occur in many localities throughout New South Wales, Victoria, South Australia, Tasmania and Queensland.

This pretty deer is still the most popular and widespread deer of the parks and forests of England. Originally native to central Europe, the Middle East, North Africa, Spain and Persia, this deer has found new homes throughout the world. In Australia it has adapted itself well, for it prefers open, improved pasture and

Fallow Deer

grasslands bordered by bush cover. This habitat preference, coupled with the deer's gentle manner, has influenced many property owners to introduce them to their farms.

Fallow deer have many features which have ensured their popularity. Generally they do not range far, nor do they do much damage provided their numbers are kept in check. They are considered an attractive animal and their distinctive palmated antlers are prized by hunters. The meat, or venison as it is termed, is also sought after as it is considered by many to be the tastiest and most flavoursome of all.

This medium sized deer is larger than the hog deer and smaller than the red deer. Their antlers set them apart from all other deer introduced to Australia. Rather than consisting of branching cylindrical and pointed tines like most deer, the antlers of the fallow reach up and end in a flat-bladed palm, the outer rear edge of which has many fine points.

The fallow also differ from all other deer in the wide colour range of their coats, which vary from almost pure white, to red with white spots, or black-backed with greyish fawn underparts. Their coats seem to change with the season; usually they are a much lighter shade in summer and turn darker in winter so that the spots almost disappear.

Another distinction the fallow enjoy is that the male is the only one of his kind to be correctly called a 'buck', and the female is known as a 'doe' rather than a hind or cow, as are other female deer. The newborn fallow deer are termed 'fawns', whereas the young of other deer are 'calves'.

The fallow are very similar to most other deer in their habits. They are a gregarious deer; when undisturbed they are often found in very large herds with females of all ages and juvenile males. The adult males tend to live together in bachelor groups separate from the main herd. For most of the year the herd is usually led by an experienced and aging female. This matriarch seems to have control over all matters concerning the herd. At her command, they rise from rest as one, feed in the direction she determines, and rest again at her example.

During March and April, the mating season, or rut, begins. It is then that the mature bucks become dominant by attracting harems of females from the herd and establishing their separate breeding territory.

Throughout this time the bucks emit their challenging call which, in the fallow's case, is a very deep grunt or cough. It is quite distinctive and differs from the call of other deer. The doe has a call, although it is mostly used when danger threatens and is more of an alarm bark, similar to a cough to clear the throat. She usually stamps her front feet at the same time as a warning to others, then prances off in the typical stiff-legged gait of the breed, showing the delicate grace for which this species is renowned.

Deer are cautious animals, and the fallow exemplify this. When feeding in poor light conditions they tend to frequent more open areas which offer them some measure of protection. They obtain the bulk of their diet by grazing, then, as the daylight becomes brighter, they seek the cover of the bush edge and browse on leaves of bushes and shrubs. Deer are always alert, and possess incredibly keen eyesight, hearing and sense of smell, compared with most other animals.

The fallow are the deer Australians are most likely to see in the wild. This species is also proving very popular for deer farming, both for export venison and to provide breeding stock which hunting organisations purchase so as to ensure trophy shooting for their members, thus introducing the fallow to new areas.

Sambar Deer

Sambar deer differ in many ways from the other deer species introduced to Australia.

Firstly, they are the largest; mature stags stand more than one and a half metres at the shoulder and are of a powerful build, weighing up to 250 kg. They are similar in body size to a large steer. The females or hinds, whilst capable of attaining the same height and weight of the stags, are somewhat finer in appearance.

We normally think of deer as being timid and graceful creatures, but the sambar stag has a truly wild, arrogant and aggressive air about him.

The sambar, almost entirely nocturnal, are the most secretive and elusive of all deer. Should they become aware of your presence, considering themselves to have been undetected, they will steal away with barely a sound, belying their large size.

If, on the other hand, they are surprised, they will burst from cover with a deep loud grunt, and then crash off through the dense undergrowth, smashing all in their way.

Much can be understood of any introduced creature's habits and behaviour when consideration is given to the relationship of predator and prey in their native land.

Being a native of Asia, including India, Malaya, Sumatra and most of South-East Asia (where they inhabit tropical rainforest and to a lesser extent the monsoon forest), the sambar have developed their extraordinary senses and stealth to avoid their predator in this region, the tiger. Capable of incredible stealth and having the most perfect of camouflage, the tiger is ample cause for the sambar to be ever alert.

Both female and young male sambar are a uniform darkish brown, apart from the white underside of the relatively long tail. The sambar, like all deer when alarmed, raise the tail like a white flag as an effective warning signal to others. Only the old stags show a variation from the common brown colour, in that they sometimes appear purple/black with a tan/orange coloured mane or ruff which extends from the cheeks to the lower part of the neck.

The sambar has an unusual coat, in that it is very coarse, consisting of long bristly hairs, each with a silver tip. The coat is relatively sparse, sometimes with the white skin showing through in places where the hair has been rubbed off, suggesting that the sambar sees little direct sunlight. In fact they show a distinct preference for dark shaded areas.

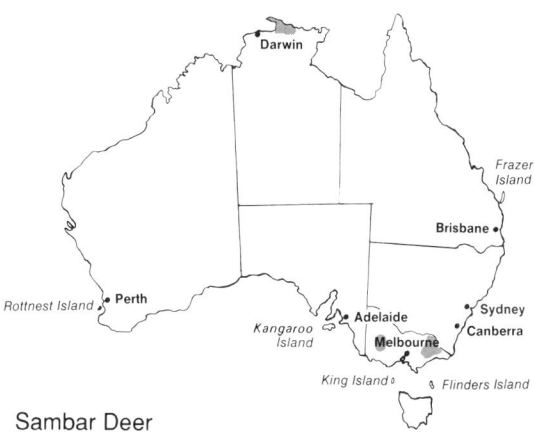

Sambar Deer

The sambar deer in Australia are found in the Northern Territory, on the Coburg Peninsula north of Darwin, and in Victoria, in both the west and east of the state. In western Victoria, small herds exist in the Grampians and in a small state forest near Ballarat. However, in the

Great Dividing Range of eastern Victoria, sambar are found in good numbers and are continuing to spread throughout the mountains and valleys of the large area of Gippsland.

They were originally released into only a small area of swampland some distance to the east of Melbourne. But devasting bushfires in 1939 and later in 1967, which engulfed their previous range, caused them to seek new country. They have also been aided in their spread by hunters using running hounds. Such hunting has the effect of chasing the deer many, many kilometres, for the sambar never give up easily. The deer escaping capture then sometimes establish themselves in new areas.

The future of the sambar in Australia seems assured, as they are widely dispersed and the habitat seems entirely suitable. The rugged ranges in eastern Victoria, which have innumerable steep-sided valleys and warm moist gullies interspersed with streams, springs and rivers, are not unlike their original homeland. Here, in what appear ideal surroundings, they form their separate groups, usually of around six to eight animals, which then occupy a gully in relative seclusion from other groups. The sambar do form large herds; in fact, each group seems to exist entirely on its own. The group seems to regulate itself, deciding when mating takes place, what period antlers are grown (as the males of all deer species grow a new set of antlers each year), and when young will be born. Unlike almost all other species of deer, they do not have a particular and regular time of the year when such things happen.

The sambar have found a niche in Australia without affecting other creatures to any great extent, and as their damage to crops, forests and other areas is considered to be slight, they are not unwelcome here.

Hog Deer

Since the hog deer's arrival in Australia, it has found our coastal climate and vegetation much to its liking. Hog deer would feel at home virtually anywhere around Australia's vast coastline and yet, surprisingly, they only occur on a narrow strip of the south-east coast of Victoria, and adjacent offshore islands. They enjoy this region's many reedy marshes, mangroves and ti-tree swamps, and occasionally they can be seen on the sandy shorelines of the ocean beaches, seeking kelp and seaweed.

The hog deer is the smallest of our introduced deer. As the name implies, they are hog-like, being short (about 65 cm), long in the back and wide in the loin with short legs. They do not possess the grace of movement of most other deer species.

The hog deer show a seasonal variation of coat colour from dark rust brown in winter, to a summer coat of creamy fawn, often with faint white spots. Their colour does not afford them effective camouflage in this country, although it certainly would in the dry high grass swamps of their native home lands of India and Burma. Although they were introduced to Sri Lanka long ago, they are now restricted to the Ganges River delta of India. This vast

Hog Deer

and largely uninhabited area consists of a maze of mangrove swamps and swamp forest which is flooded twice daily by the tides of this massive river system.

So rather than live in open grassy hill country, as most other deer species seem to prefer, the hog deer are never far from water. Rather than eat normal grass, they choose instead to eat fresh water swamp herbage and, more importantly, plants growing in or near salt or brackish water. It is these plants which have absorbed some level of salt that the hog deer seek, whether it be in tidal rivers, estuaries, or in lakes and swamps with salt-laden soils that are sometimes found a good distance inland from the sea.

It seems hog deer require a high level of salt, as the areas in which they choose to live, both in Australia and in their native range, are of this type. In fact when in captivity, hog deer develop a wasting of the hind quarters which severely restricts their normal movement, and may in part be due to a deficiency of salt.

As hog deer are only semi-nocturnal, they are quite often encountered feeding in open clearings during mid-morning and mid-afternoon. They graze busily without being constantly on the alert for danger, unlike most other deer. However, in the low scrub of silver tussock, sword grass and bracken fern, they are difficult to see and approach. Should they become alarmed, they will give either a shrill whistle or a bark like a deep cough before scattering in all directions, either crashing through the undergrowth or silently creeping away with their head held low, the stags with their 50 cm antlers lying back along their neck, an unusual habit in Asiatic deer.

Hog deer do not form herds, preferring instead to lead a near solitary existence, although they may sometimes be seen in small groups in prime grazing areas. So rather than being in concentrated pockets, they are more widely distributed throughout this coastal region. Whilst their total numbers are unknown, it is thought that they are rapidly declining, particularly in areas of easy public access on the mainland of Victoria, as in some of these areas they now seem to be extremely rare.

The National Parks Service, which administers much of the hog deer's range, found from research that they live in harmony with their habitat, both in regard to the vegetation and the wide variety of wildlife which shares its range. It was found that the deer could happily coexist with other animals, notably large kangaroos, wallabies and emus, which share the grazing areas. It was noted that the deer did not appear to put heavy pressure on the available food supply, nor did they disturb the habitat to an extent which was beyond management control.

Rusa Deer

The rusa deer, being a lover of the rich plant growth that borders the thick rainforest of South-East Asia, Java, Timor and many other neighbouring islands of that region, has also found a new home in this country.

This medium sized deer is a very close cousin to the sambar; they are somewhat similar in appearance and share many of the same habits. The rusa, however, is smaller than its relative. Rusa stags rarely weigh more than 110 kg or exceed one metre at the shoulder. Their body colour differs from the sambar; it is lighter brown, with white underparts, chest and chin.

As the rusa and the sambar show a preference for the same type of habitat, they were often both released into the same areas in Australia, particularly in parts of Victoria and the Northern Territory. They readily interbreed with one another, which results in offspring more like the sambar than the rusa. This has caused confusion between the two species to the point where it is difficult to

cont'd on page 33

Blackbuck antelope, native to India, were introduced to Western Australia.

Above: Red Deer stag. Imported as an animal to hunt, it has not become a pest.

Below: Young fallow deer. This species is by far the most widespread of those introduced.

Sambar stag. The largest and most powerfully built of all introduced deer can weigh 250 kg.

European red fox. An intelligent, opportunistic predator: declared vermin by governments.

Of all the creatures introduced to Australia, the European rabbit has had the greatest impact.

Above: Typical damage caused by the rabbit – an extensive warren with scarcely any vegetation nearby.

Below: The cane toad, a native of South America, was introduced to control beetles in sugar cane.

Brumbies; mare and foal. Fortunately much of the cruelty once involved in catching such horses is a thing of the past.

Above: Mob of inland brumbies. Many of their forebears escaped breeding programmes to provide horses for the army.

Below: Massive wide horns and a solid mud-caked body typify the water buffalo, an import from Asia.

Above: The feral pig is always unpredictable at close quarters. Purposely released, they readily adapted to the wild.

Below: The strong tusks of the feral pig make it well equipped to tear up burrows and dig up plants.

Above: This splendid billy goat with his impressive horns and beard could become part of the new mohair industry.

Below: Goats were released to provide future sources of fresh meat and milk for victims of shipwreck, sealers and whalers.

Above: The dingo is not a new wild animal but Australians have not yet accepted it as a native species.

Below: As appealing as any pup, this little dingo will doubtless grow into its large ears.

Above: The starling, a town bird from Europe, is boisterous and aggressive.

Below: The juvenile starling looks quite different from the adult bird. It is a uniform shade of pale grey-brown.

Above: Unfortunately poison is still required to be used to control feral dogs and pigs.

Below: This huge feral dog was responsible for killing many sheep, lambs and calves before it was shot.

Above: The blackbird was one of the first birds imported from Europe for its song.

Below: A close relative of the blackbird, the song thrush was released along with its favourite food, the garden snail.

Above: The ringneck pheasant, imported for sport, was introduced late last century.

Below: Chicks and eggs of the ground-dwelling ringneck pheasant are well camouflaged.

Above: The author in the field, using a shoulder-mounted 400mm lens.

Below: The future concerns will be restoration, management and control. The challenge will be to find better methods.

positively identify rusa in areas it shares with the sambar.

The true rusa deer today is found in the Gulf Country of Queensland and on a number of the islands off the coast, as well as in a number of localities in both eastern and western Victoria. However, the best known herd is in the Royal National Park near Sydney in New South Wales.

Most rusa shot in Australia come from this park; many hunters seeking the deer's 60 cm antlers prefer to risk prosecution rather than incur the expense of hunting them legally in New Guinea, New Caledonia and the many other islands to which the rusa has been introduced. To legally hunt or even see the elusive rusa in other wild or remote areas of Australia requires knowledge and considerable skill in the art of stalking as well as physical endurance by those who seek them.

Although the rusa seek heavy cover in almost inpenetrable scrub where hunting pressure is high; when left alone they prefer to feed in semi-open country as they appear to be grazers rather than browsers.

The rusa, like all deer species, and in fact like most grazing animals, are ruminants or cud chewers. These animals have no front teeth on the upper jaw, enabling them to bite off grass more closely to the ground, but preventing them from chewing their food properly. Nature has equipped them instead with four stomachs, so that they can derive the utmost nutritional value from what they eat. As their diet consists of all plant material (most of which has tough and fibrous tissues), the rusa only briefly chew what they have bitten off before swallowing it. They continue to feed in this way until their first stomach is full. They then choose a place to rest where the food can be chewed a second time, so that it is more thoroughly broken down. This process is achieved by means of a small ball of food being passed from the first stomach back to the mouth where it is rolled and ground thoroughly by the strong back teeth. This ball is swallowed again and then passes to each of the other stomachs in turn, so they can complete digestion. This cud chewing process is carried on until the first stomach is emptied; then, after a short rest, the deer will begin feeding again. It is little wonder that they spend as much as eight hours each day of their average life span of fifteen years simply eating or chewing.

A timid and wary animal, the rusa deer is sure to have a long future in this, its new home.

Rusa Deer

Chital Deer

The chital or axis deer, with its reddish brown coat covered with permanent white spots, is considered by many to be the most attractive deer in the world. For this reason, as well as to provide sport, it was brought from its native India by our early settlers and set free in many parts of Australia.

Our British forefathers were familiar with the chital deer from their colony of India, or had admired it in the parklands of England, where it had been introduced and is still commonly found.

33

They considered this beautiful deer would be a pleasant addition to Australia's wildlife and set about making many importations and releases, yet today it is the rarest of all our imported deer. Although it was liberated in numerous localities in nearly every state, it is now only found in good numbers on private property in central Queensland where the deer's long-term survival can now be guaranteed.

The chital failed to establish itself in most other areas, because they were mercilessly hunted from the moment of their release. These deer do not run at man's approach and their habit of preferring to feed in open country during daylight made them easy targets. Failures also occurred, particularly in southern Australia, where the chital were often released in cold, dense eucalypt forest and bushland. These areas couldn't have been more unsuitable for the chital as in their homeland their habitat is the humid monsoon deciduous forest close to open savannah grasslands.

The northern monsoon belt of Australia should have been ideal for them, and although there are occasional reports of them, particularly on Coburg and Cape York Peninsulas, the sightings have not been confirmed.

The chital were once the most common deer in India, occupying vast areas from the foothills of the Himalayas to the island of Sri Lanka. Today, however, since they have been hunted excessively like their predator the tiger, they are becoming very rare. Both now only live in remote regions or on wildlife reserves in India. Another cause of their reduced numbers is the changes brought by man to their habitat in clearing forest and placing cattle on available grassland. Cattle not only compete with the deer for food but also infect them with tuberculosis and rinderpest disease.

Unfortunately, the chital is just hanging on in its homeland. The world can ill afford to lose this handsome deer so one hopes that perhaps some will remain in northern Australia.

Blackbuck Antelope

This small Indian antelope, which stands only 70 cm at the shoulder and weighs about 40 kg, has a striking appearance.

Chital Deer

The adult males have a distinctive black and white colour, with spiralling horns growing up to about 60 cm long. Many consider them to be one of nature's most attractive grazing animals.

When considering the variety and vastness of the Australian outback, it would seem that there is ample ideal habitat for the blackbuck. So it is surprising that they were only introduced to one location in Western Australia. Today blackbuck numbers are extremely small, and its long term future is doubtful.

Blackbuck Antelope

Sadly the blackbuck suffers the same fate in its native India, where although it was once the most abundant hoofed wild animal, it is now extremely rare. Its decline in India was brought about by people's excessive use of its habitat. Trees and shrubs were cut for firewood and domestic animals over-grazed the cleared land. Unmanaged hunting in its native range over the years has also taken its toll of this speedy and graceful creature. The blackbuck had little hope of outrunning Emperor Akba's one thousand trained cheetahs, who were used exclusively for hunting them for sport.

Fortunately they were introduced to the USA, where there are now more of them than there are in India. They are cared for and managed successfully; but for this, the world would certainly lose a beautiful antelope.

Fox

The European red fox was released into Victoria during the 1860s to provide sport for the 'well-to-do' in the English tradition.

Following the goldrush of the mid-nineteenth century, many settlers became wealthy from farming and other activities and they began to pursue the lifestyle of English country squires. They formed hunting packs of hounds, prepared many fine horses and equipped themselves with top hats, horns and 'Tally-Hos'. The native wildlife, when confronted with these new and totally foreign methods of hunting, simply stood and stared, offering no semblance of sport.

The fox was imported to fill this sporting need. It was also thought that it might provide some future natural control of the rabbit, an earlier arrival in our land, and an inhabitant that later proved to be extremely troublesome in some areas.

Since its arrival, the fox has adapted so well to this country that it is now by far the most numerous and widespread of all the larger introduced wild animals. It now occurs in great numbers in every state except Tasmania, where each time foxes were released they were quickly killed by the authorities and by those with a stake in the welfare of the island state's sheep flocks and poultry runs.

The number of foxes and their distribution throughout Australia is surprising, considering the enormous hunting pressure they have constantly been under. Hunting in the English traditional method has given way to the spotlight, trap and gun. It is not the sport that foxes provide now so much as the valuable skins, and although some half a million pelts find their way to the eastern states' markets each year, it hardly makes a dent in fox numbers.

Declared vermin by governments, despised by sheep graziers and poultry farmers, as well as being mercilessly hunted for their valuable skins, foxes have spread out from populated areas to avoid this relentless pursuit. The fox now not only occupies our farmlands, but also the highest snow-covered mountains, forests and most of our coastal areas as well as much of the saltbush and mulga country of the outback. As if dissatisfied with all of

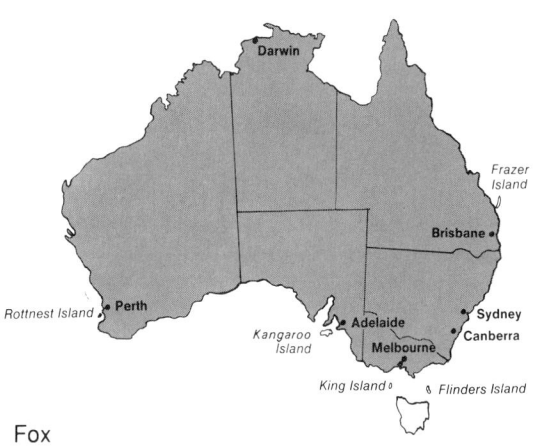

Fox

this, however, the fox will cheekily appear at night in our major cities and towns to raid the garbage dumps and schoolyards in search of a meal.

The fox is a member of the dog family (order Canidae). The male fox is called a dog and the female a vixen. Foxes share many of their habits with our domestic pets, notably the burying of excess food in scattered locations. The fox can bark; it has a peculiar raspy tone. It is usually only heard at night or during mating time when it also utters the weirdest of sounds, a mixture of yelping, crying and wailing. Similarly, dog foxes mark their territory as our pets do, by urinating on plants and other objects as a means of telling others of their kind that this territory is occupied, and where its boundaries are located.

The young are not born killers. At birth they weigh only a hundred grams, and their fluffy chocolate brown or smoky grey fur and blue eyes make them look more like kittens than foxes. It is their mother that patiently teaches them to develop the necessary skills of hunting and survival; for not only must the young learn to eat, but at the same time they must recognise their enemies — eagles, hawks, dingoes, and people and their dogs. This is why the fox is very much a creature of the night, preferring to spend the daylight hours asleep in the security of a rocky outcrop, fern patch or creek bed.

In the past, because of generations of folklore and a probable lack of understanding, we were wrongly led to believe that the fox was a bloodthirsty and insatiable killer of poultry and lambs. That foxes are sly, cunning and efficient killers is undisputable, however modern detailed studies have shown the fox to be an intelligent, opportunist predator and scavenger. Foxes enjoy a surprisingly diverse diet. Being omnivores, they eat virtually anything from lizards, snakes, frogs, fish, earthworms, snails, spiders, grubs and beetles to other relished morsels including apples, pears, plums, blackberries and even cabbages.

It is hard to excuse their killing of our native wildlife; in some areas they must take a heavy toll. Farmers of course will not excuse them for killing healthy lambs, although they only do this rarely. Mostly they take lambs abandoned by their mothers, so weakened and starving they are easy prey. During lambing there are many natural casualties amongst the flocks due to difficult births, and ewes dying; this is a bounty for the fox. In many cases the fox is accused of the actual killing, simply because the farmer sees him at the scene. Similarly, the fox entering a henhouse most probably wants only one bird and not many, as some claim, just to satisfy some unexplained blood lust. Most likely, in the pandemonium and panic that results from their presence, they snap in a confined space at everything in range, thereby killing many in the process. It is little wonder that they have not endeared themselves to the farmer.

Few animals could withstand the constant harassment the fox experiences, and yet still appear in such numbers. They can be thankful for two things; first their adaptability, for they are considered the third most adaptable creature in the world after man and rabbit. Secondly, furriers favour them; by placing a value on their beautiful yellow to reddish brown pelt, they assist the fox in its survival by pleading with hunters to only snare them in the winter months when skins are of premium quality. The fox, being a summer breeder, is able to take advantage of this respite, by replacing its numbers in the non-hunting season.

Such is the nature of the fox, with its reputation for slyness and cunning, that it seems able to resist most control measures man has dealt it.

Rabbit

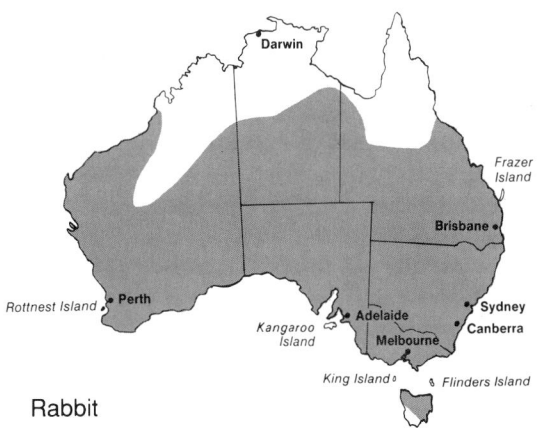

Rabbit

Of all the wild animals that have been introduced to Australia, none has had the lasting impact of the European rabbit.

Rabbits first arrived in Sydney with Governor Phillip's fleet in 1788. They were kept in hutches on board ship as part of the fresh food supply; it was common European practice. Little did anyone realise that with later deliberate introductions, especially during the 1830s and in 1860, the European rabbit would prove to be the most formidable agricultural pest in Australia.

Though rabbits were no real problem when first released in small numbers for sport and for variety in people's diet, they soon spread. Their widening distribution was also greatly assisted by people who took them almost everywhere and then released them.

Rabbits very quickly adapted themselves and bred as only rabbits can, to become a population estimated at eight hundred million during the height of their 'reign of terror', which lasted some seventy years (1880 to 1950). There were six times as many rabbits as there were sheep. There were one hundred rabbits for every man, woman, and child in Australia.

It seemed that there was not a place in Australia that rabbits did not occupy at least for a short time. They spread out

over the dry flat plains of the outback, the hot arid inland deserts, our timbered and snow-capped mountains, the beaches and sand dunes of our coast and offshore islands, as well as everywhere on the vast grazing lands of this country.

Rabbits ate everything before them, not only grasses, but shrubs and bushes of every size. They ate bark off trees and killed them. They even ate windblown trees that were lying on the ground. It was said at the time that they were seen to move across the landscape as a sea of grey.

Their effect on this country was catastrophic. There was no grass left for stock, and this brought the grazing industry to its knees, which in turn had a drastic effect on the nation's economy. They caused erosion of every type, on a scale that was beyond imagination. They ate plants so thoroughly and continuously that their roots died, and so no longer held the soil together. The wind and the rain were able to move the soil about at will, affecting vast areas that still have not recovered. River courses were changed as the soil was washed away by rains and seasonal flooding.

The rabbits' presence changed the environment dramatically; their impact was incredibly widespread. Not only did they deny food for our animals, but also for our native grazers such as kangaroos and wallabies. They ate the cover wildlife needed for rest, shelter and breeding. Their constant chewing stopped grasses from growing and seeding, causing many native birds to go hungry. They ate shrubs and bushes so that proper nest sites were hard for birds to find.

Of course the rabbit brought hardship, heartbreak and ruin to countless families on the land. Their land was no longer productive so there was no income. This in turn meant that in time there was a seemingly endless stream of those leaving their devastated properties for the cities and towns in search of work. The suffering, hardship and damage the rabbit has caused in Australia can never be overstated.

Why was it that this little fluffy grey animal from Europe was able to cause such havoc in this country when we obtained it from the green fields of England? One would assume that rabbits would not like it here, considering that our climate and vegetation are vastly different. The answer is that England is not their true home, they had been introduced there centuries earlier.

Their natural range is the Mediterranean region, where the climate is similar to our own. They rarely, if ever, get out of hand in their home range, for the ground is more rocky and it is more closely settled by people. In Britain and around the Mediterranean, the farms are relatively small, and heavily stocked with other grazing animals which compete with rabbits for food. The farmers on these small holdings know each paddock intimately and keep rabbit numbers in check. In Australia, however, some of the properties are the size of whole European countries. Here rabbits could breed and spread unnoticed. The soils here were ideal for burrowing and there was not the same heavy competition from other grazers. The more temperate and stable climate suited them better, as they usually had grass all year round. In their European homeland the grass does not grow in autumn and winter, and this acts as a natural restriction on breeding.

Sheep made a considerable contribution to the spread of rabbits throughout Australia, as the sheep's habit of close grazing made the feed the ideal length for the rabbits to eat. Rabbits do not like long grass; in fact long grass is the greatest deterrent to the increase in numbers and spread of rabbits. At the time of the rabbit's new found freedom, Australia's sheep flocks were approaching enormous numbers, some one hundred and twenty million. They were grazing everywhere, opening up country that would have been unsuitable for rabbits before the sheep arrived.

With feelings running high against the pest for so long, it is no wonder that few people have bothered to look closely at the rabbit's behaviour. Yet its habits and amazingly complex lifestyle deserve a closer examination.

For example, there were reports of people seeing black rabbits, whilst others were yellow or a sandy colour, in addition to the most common colour known as 'agouti'. The variation in colours did not indicate different species, as was commonly thought, but was merely nature's way of allowing the animal to achieve a colour that most suited its surroundings. Black rabbits were most often seen in dense areas in mountain forest country, particularly in parts of the Great Dividing Range and in areas of Tasmania, whereas sandy-coloured ones mainly inhabited the sand dunes and beaches in coastal regions.

Because rabbits are burrowing animals which may spend up to half their lives underground, they have developed a highly complex social system, which enables them to get on well together.

Their social group begins to develop when a female or doe chooses an area that is to her liking, with both adequate feed available and ground that is suitable for burrowing. With the onset of the breeding season, which is usually from late winter to late summer, the does begin to attract interest from the bucks or males who assist in digging the burrow in the area she has chosen. Being social animals, these areas attract more rabbits, so numerous burrows are dug by others, developing into a network of tunnels called a warren. This may cover an area as small as four metres square or be so extensive as to cover several hectares and contain hundreds of rabbits.

The warren is controlled by a number of dominant bucks, who have chosen females and burrows. The bucks begin to establish the territory they have claimed by depositing strong odours from a gland under the chin around their boundary line. They are prepared to defend their territory against all comers. Should a rival cross this line, fierce fights develop; the bucks bite and tear each other's fur out with their sharp teeth and claws. These disputes usually occur at the time of the formation of the colony, and once settled, a relatively quiet, orderly and well behaved society is developed and maintained. Each rabbit in the warren knows every other as an individual, each with a slightly different personality and each with a place in the order of things. It is nature's way of ensuring development and prosperity of the colony as a whole.

After mating, the does gather dry grass

and, by mixing it with fur pulled from their chests, they make a soft bed in the blind end of the burrow. The tiny sixty gram kittens are born here; they are helpless creatures which begin life blind and deaf and without hair or fur. Within just two weeks they are covered in a coat of soft fur and their bright eyes are ready to discover the world outside their dark and cramped burrow.

Nature has equipped the rabbit with the ablity to control the number of young born depending on the availability of food. In times of plentiful feed the number in a litter may be as high as ten, whereas if food is in short supply, the litter can be reduced to only two. It is not only the rabbit's capacity to produce large litters in times of plenty that makes it such a prolific animal, but its capacity for numerous short pregnancies. It only takes thirty days from the time of mating for a doe to bear young, and she is capable of producing a litter every month of the usual eight month breeding season. In a single season she could, in ideal conditions, produce up to eighty young and some of these would be having young of their own. Generally, however, twenty to twenty-five young per season would be considered normal. Not all of these would survive and reach maturity, as many of the young are lost to predators and sometimes the doe is unable to feed them all due to lack of food. Unseasonal cold snaps or heavy rains which fill their burrows also take their toll.

Rabbits are probably the most prolific breeders of all animals and nature has provided a unique means of controlling their numbers—stress. In situations where rabbits have exhausted the available food supply, they must either seek out new areas, thus widening their distribution, or remain with abnormal competition. Uneasiness begins to take over the previously happy society. Fights and squabbles break out amongst friends and many does fail to bear live young. Because of inadequate feed and lack of rest, a number of diseases begin to take a toll on weakened members. Others, only partially affected, lack the strength to compete with those that are fit for the food that remains and so many just give up and show a complete lack of will to live. This stress factor impinging on the rabbit's behaviour is an effective means of controlling overcrowding. These population crashes are a natural thing, and are just one way of nature ensuring the survival of the fittest.

The rabbit may be one of the animal world's more interesting creatures, but by wreaking such havoc in Australia, it caused most people to despise it and employ every possible means to eradicate it. Rabbits were killed in their thousands. People hit them with sticks, trapped them, drowned them, set dogs on them, placed cats and ferrets down their burrows, shot them, poisoned them and dug up their warrens. Some land owners even resorted to using highly toxic cyanide gas, placing their own lives at great risk, but the rabbits held their own. At the same time governments were offering a 'life's fortune' to anyone who could come up with the answer to the rabbit problem.

Not until the Second World War did there appear to be an answer to this vexing problem. Dame Jean McNamara hit upon the solution when she learnt that a viral disease known as myxomatosis was killing large numbers of South American rabbits. It was enthusiastically claimed that this disease could be spread by mosquitoes and so infect large numbers of rabbits in a short time. So highly infectious and lethal was this virus that it had a fatality rate of ninety-nine per cent. Most importantly it only fatally affected rabbits.Unfortunately, years passed before the government was prepared to listen and learn of the great possibilities of this virus as a means of rabbit control.

Once introduced in 1950, myxomatosis had such a devastating effect on rabbit numbers that just three years later it had reduced the rabbit population to almost nil. This potent and highly successful control agent produced results that could previously only have been dreamt of.

Before myxomatosis was introduced, however, the American mouse and rat poison 1080 had been found to have dramatic results on the rabbit. A machine was invented to chop up carrots by the tonne. The carrots were then laced with 1080, making a bait which was laid in trails that criss-crossed the whole country. These tempting baits were only intended for rabbits but, of course, many other creatures ate them, or the carcases of those that had eaten them, and they died too. The use of 1080 caused far too great a toll to be taken of our native animals and birds.

Fencing was another measure used to control the rabbit. Many fences were joined together to create the longest netting fence in the world. Later this was increased in height in an attempt to stop the dingo.

The rabbit is largely responsible for our feral cat problem, as cats were bred in thousands and released by the government in an ill conceived attempt at rabbit control.

Some people made a good deal of money from rabbits. In the old days processors from the city arrived on properties with their teams of rabbiters and refrigerated trailers made from converted mail vans and bookmaker buses. Many thousands of people were able to feed and clothe themselves and their families with money made from rabbits when there was no other income to be had during the Great Depression of the 1930s. These people have fond memories of the rabbit, and it was ironic that the money they made came from sending the rabbits back to England as a much sought after meat.

Nowadays, however, apart from sporadic outbreaks, rabbits are considered to be under control, although they continue to take up a good deal of time for those who must keep a check on them. The majority of farmers, who once hated them, seem now to be not unhappy at having a few rabbits on the place.

European Hare

The European hare was another animal imported from England for sport. It came in at about the same time as the rabbit, early last century. Hares readily adapted to Australia and spread throughout areas of gently sloping hills and open grassland in Queensland, New South Wales and Victoria. They limited their range to the west of South Australia on the Nullarbor Plain. They occur on Tasmania's low country and on numerous Bass Strait islands.

They built up into such numbers that in some areas it was common for small parties of shooters to bag hundreds in a single day's outing.

The hare has always been something of a delicacy on the tables of Europe. It wasn't long before enterprising trappers established a ready export market, thus assisting the landowners who were complaining that the hares liked their

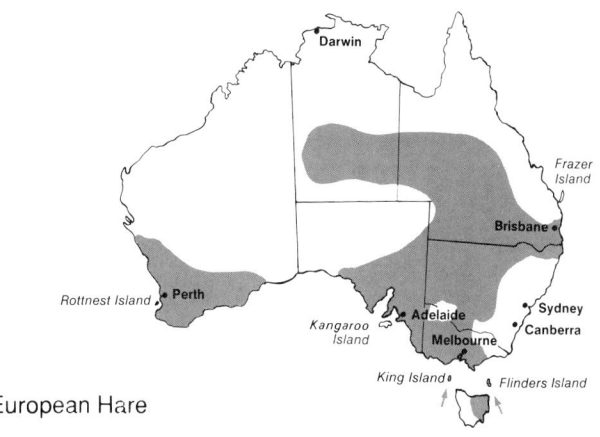

European Hare

crops of oats, clover, and turnips. Hares competed with sheep and cattle for the grass of grazing lands as they enjoy longer grass than rabbits.

Although having a somewhat similar appearance to the rabbit at first glance, the hare is a very different animal. It is almost twice the size of the rabbit, and weighs about 3½ kg (especially females, which are larger than the males). They have a rangy, athletic appearance with long powerful legs, a coat of rich tawny brown, very long white whiskers, and of course, their most distinguishing feature, their long black-tipped ears.

Rather than have young in a burrow, the hare will choose a position beside a tussock, log, or rock so as to provide cover as well as to be out of the wind, and simply scratch a shallow depression in the ground and line it with soft fur plucked from the chest. In this 'form' or 'squat', from two to eight young are born. They are called 'leverets'. They are born with eyes open, they have fur, and the ability to run almost immediately. The hare is a solitary animal for most of the year. However 'Mad as a March hare' is an apt English expression to describe their antics and comical behaviour when they gather in large groups at the beginning of the mating season (March in England, around September in Australia).

Hares have only four to six litters each year and most commonly raise only two young per litter. The hare never became the universal problem to the farmers that the rabbit was. Not only do hares have a lower breeding rate, but they and their young live above ground, so they are far more susceptible to predators and the effects of people. They suffer many losses as the farmers' machinery works the ground, particularly at harvest time.

Hares are strange creatures in that, whilst they are constantly alert, they can sometimes be quiety approached until you can almost touch them; a rigid fear seems to grip them so that they appear unable to move. Perhaps it is just that they have great faith in their speed, for it is likely that the hares are aware of your approach long before you see them. Their ability to blend in with almost flat ground is truly amazing. Often it appears that they can almost be stepped on before they will seemingly explode from underfoot. They then accelerate into their familiar zigzag running retreat, or into a wonderfully smooth, economical lope which belies their true speed.

The legendary abilities of the hare have made them the quarry for coursing with greyhounds and other hunting dogs, a cruel sport now thankfully banned. (Many of the organisers weren't really sporting minded as they often netted off the hare's escape.) In open country, however, the hare, with bursts of speed up to sixty kilometres per hour and the ability to make sudden sharp turns, proves the better of all but the very best of dogs. Regardless of how far and how hard he is pressed by the hounds, the hare will almost always unerringly return to the spot in the paddock where he was first flushed.

Although hares occur in high enough numbers in some areas to allow continued exports to Europe, one usually has trouble finding them these days. This is not because of direct measures by man, although hares do pick up 1080 baits left out for the rabbit, but rather their numbers are affected by modern intensive farming methods which no longer leave sufficient cover for them. However they will most certainly survive, for they are most adaptable.

Cane Toad

The South American cane toad must be one of the most unlikely and unusual creatures to be deliberately brought to this country and set free. The Queensland Government introduced cane toads from Hawaii in 1935. They had been introduced there, too, as they have been to all countries growing sugar cane, because they were shown to be of some effect in controlling two species of cane beetles which had been inadvertently introduced with the sugar cane plant, and which cause serious damage to this important crop.

Cane toads had initial success as a control agent in Australia where, however, they bred alarmingly. It was not long before the cane toads spread out of the cane fields. They are not frogs, which usually remain in or near water, but ground-dwelling toads capable of travelling considerable distances. They now occupy almost all of the tropical coastal belt of New South Wales and Queensland. They are moving westwards towards Darwin, colonising at the rate of twenty-seven kilometres a year.

The cane toad is large and heavily built; it varies in colour from dull green to tan, has an exceptionally warty and irregularly marked skin, and short but very strong legs.

When they first colonise an area, they grow very large, commonly attaining 230 mm in length and weighing 1.25 kg, although for some reason they decrease markedly in size as their numbers build up.

The cane toad is omnivorous, it eats almost everything, including insects of every type, centipedes, scorpions, mice, small snakes and virtually anything else that will pass through its jaws. Its impact on our native wildlife is incalculable.

Cane toads are prolific breeders

throughout their relatively long life of fifteen years. During this time, the females may deposit forty thousand eggs per season, the tadpoles emerging after three or four days. Incredibly, males are able to undergo a sex change to become fertile females.

Their prodigious breeding rate, coupled with their ability to eat almost anything, has allowed the cane toad to increase in numbers at an exceptional rate in this country and to spread rapidly into habitat that is ideally suited to it. Many predators such as foxes, dingoes, eagles, hawks and snakes have naturally been enticed by what appeared to be a new and abundant food source. However, eating the toad has dire consequences, for it is poisonous to all that come in contact with it. Very toxic venom is exuded from large glands on

Cane Toad

either side of the rear of the cane toad's head. Predators, when grabbing the toad in their mouth, suffer almost instant pain and although they quickly let the toad go, thus saving its life, it is often too late to save their own. It is also claimed that the cane toad can squirt this venom some distance and affect the eyes of those that annoy it. Even the poison that remains in the bodies of dead toads affects those that handle them. When the venom is in water, it will affect fish and other creatures. Domestic cats and dogs are frequently killed and it is claimed that humans have died after eating them.

The toads usually seek cover during the day and so they are most often seen at night in open areas such as suburban lawns or on roadways and streets, particularly after rain. They occasionally gather in groups of a dozen or more, either close to water in the breeding season, where they can be heard croaking enthusiastically to attract mates, or sometimes they gather in the light beneath street lamps where there are many insects to be easily caught. Toads will happily sit by commercial hives of honey bees and eat them in large quantities. They have forced beekeepers to re-design hives.

The resourceful toad also enjoys sitting under garden sprinklers, having a dip in a swimming pool on a hot day, and checking household garbage regularly for potato peelings and table scraps. Some toads know the regular feed times of neighbourhood dogs, and it's a sight to see a dog gulping its food whilst trying to kick away toads intent on sharing the meal.

Toads have frustrated the efforts of authorities in some areas who are trying to introduce dung beetles in an attempt to dispose of cattle dung. No sooner are the beetles released than the cane toads consume them.

Most people are loathe to handle the cane toad; however, many children have been rewarded by collecting thousands of them for worthy charities, who in turn sell them to universities and schools Australia-wide where they are used by biology students for dissection. Until the advent of more recent procedures, the cane toad was also useful to medical science for it was discovered that it could be used in a test which was a suitable and accurate means of ascertaining human pregnancy. Many thousands were used over some fifteen years for this clinical purpose. Nowadays, however, they are commercially exploited for their skin, which has found a ready market in shoes, wallets and bags.

We must be forever watchful of this adaptable foreigner and some effort must be made in the future to control the cane toad, although it will doubtless prove very difficult to do without affecting our native frogs and toads.

Rats and Mice

Australia, like almost every country in the world, was unable to prevent the accidental introduction of the common European house mouse, the European brown rat and the Asian black rat, for they have been the hidden companion of humans on most of their travels around the globe. They may have been in the holds and amongst the supplies of the ships that called at our shores before European settlement.

Whilst Australia has various native species of both rats and mice, these are creatures of the wild and attempt to avoid people. Imported rats and mice rely on people, being part and parcel of their baggage, provisions and buildings through history. Doubtless many would have landed with the first settlers; some simply swam ashore when ships were wrecked off our rocky, uncharted coasts; others hid and rode amongst the freight and materials that were unloaded at the docks of the rapidly expanding settlements. It wasn't long before these unwelcome immigrants were reported running freely wherever the settlers decided to set up house.

These three invaders forced our native rats and mice to retreat further into the bushland and away from settlements, whilst they involved themselves in their traditional role of destroying crops and stored foodstuffs, soiling and damaging buildings and spreading a multitude of diseases.

People have known of the damage these three species cause for centuries, yet all attempts to eradicate or even control them have failed. The infamous feats of these species include spreading the 'Black Death' or bubonic plague which killed millions of people throughout Europe. This disease was so devastating that ships were barred from entering ports if it was thought that rats were on board, causing many travellers to stay on board for periods of forty days or more whilst the rats were found and killed. This procedure gave rise to the word 'quarantine'. Ships are required to place cone-shaped barriers on port tie-up lines, to stop the well known traffic of these rodents along these ropes.

These animals have continued similar work in Australia; we even had an outbreak of the dreaded bubonic plague here, claiming hundred of lives. Our crops continue to suffer by their presence, and at times millions of them have swept across our grain belts, devouring all before them and forcing many farmers and townspeople to abandon their homes and holdings. The cleanups following these periodic plagues require the gathering of tonnes of carcases, monstrous mounds of them.

In good seasons these rodents can breed at a phenomenal rate, probably only equalled by the rabbit, for they are able to have eight young per litter and as they have an extremely short pregnancy (three weeks), they effortlessly cope with eight litters or more each year. At this rate, in one year a single pair can produce twelve hundred or more offspring.

The cost of these uninvited guests runs into hundreds of thousands of dollars every year. Their incessant gnawing is caused by a quirk of nature, as their bottom teeth grow at an alarming rate of

Rats and Mice

170 mm per year. They must continually wear them down by eating or they would grow grotesquely and become useless.

Rats and mice not only consume foodstuffs and crops, but they will eat lead and plastic coated wiring, causing untold electrical fires. Their teeth make short work of bricks and mortar, cardboard, wood and even tin; in fact there is little in the way of materials that their teeth cannot handle.

They rely on people to provide them with both food and shelter and although we poison them, trap them, shoot and fumigate them, they still remain with us. The Brisbane City Council still has twenty trained fox terrier dogs and their handlers whose job it is to track them down, where all else has failed. The European mouse has the Latin name of *Mus musculus*, which means 'little thief'. We shall have to continue to keep temptation out of their way and make their stealing as difficult as possible if ever we are to control them.

FERAL ANIMALS

The word 'feral' simply means 'wild', usually pertaining to animals and birds which were once domesticated and which, for a variety of reasons, have reverted to living in the wild state without the care or control of people.

Australia now has many such animals, some of which, notably goats and pigs, were possibly freed on islands off our coast long before settlement. Sea captains, whalers and sealers very often carried such hardy animals on board ships, not only as a source of fresh meat and milk, but also to release on isolated islands and lonely coasts so that they could be a source of food for anyone unfortunate enough to be shipwrecked.

Throughout our brief history, some animals have been purposely set free, some have escaped, whilst others have been abandoned and so left to fend for themselves.

From the very first days of settlement, virtually every domestic animal and bird had many opportunities to escape from pens, yards and enclosures. Even the cattle that arrived with the First Fleet strayed from their keeper and were only found again many years later; by then they had multiplied into a large herd. Their importance to the colony was paramount, yet they managed to escape. Chickens escaped, turkeys bolted, pigs ran, goats climbed out and horses and donkeys simply wandered off to feed.

Many pioneers set forth with a few animals and even fewer possessions into unknown country in an attempt to carve out a living for themselves and their families. The hardships they endured were monumental. Our seasons of cyclic droughts and floods, together with our dense bush and hard-packed untilled soils, were totally unfamiliar and difficult to deal with, let alone master.

Many settlers buckled physically and mentally under the sweat and toil of what must have seemed futile attempts to break in this new land. Many had tried to make a go of farming in areas that were entirely unsuitable for the crops they wished to grow or the stock they wished to graze. Bad seasons forced others from their selections, since they did not have the resources, equipment or money to see them through, and so they abandoned their animals and headed back to the towns and settlements in search of an easier life.

Sickness and diseases such as tuberculosis, diptheria and whooping cough were deadly in these early days. They took their toll of individuals and sometimes whole families. Simple accidents and injuries sometimes proved fatal in these isolated blocks. Without close attention and control animals wandered off or escaped into the bush. The riches promised by the goldrushes caused many to go off and seek their fortunes. Owners left their holdings, shepherds left their sheep and never returned. Others went off timber cutting and to other jobs that paid regular wages, never to return. Pack and food animals were often abandoned by explorers. Leichhardt, Giles and Grey made notes in their diaries stating that they had to abandon animals and that some animals had escaped in wild and unmapped places; camels most commonly ran wild this way.

Others escaped whilst working; carrying sleepers for the inland railways and wire and posts for the dingo fence.

Donkeys and camels carried wool and timber. Horses, too, were used as haulage and pack animals. Horses and donkeys were also often part of large breeding programmes and frequently encouraged to produce mules, which would be able to carry more than either of their parents. These animals were often set free once their allotted tasks were completed.

Many animals that we know as common farm stock have been running wild for almost two hundred years now, and some species have bred to number millions. They have adapted well in this country in areas that suit them. They live alongside our native creatures and other wildlife. Once free of the controls of domestication, they become very different creatures and show many interesting habits that they never revealed whilst on the farm.

Brumby

It was an incident of abandoning stock that gave the brumby its name. A New South Welshman of this name left his horses unattended. They simply wandered freely in his absence, and when sighted by others they were referred to as 'Brumby's horses' or 'Brumbies'. In time this name was to any horse seen wandering free.

We now have hundreds of thousands of wild horses in Australia. They occur in many parts of the Great Dividing Range in Victoria and New South Wales, the arid areas of central Australia, the rugged and

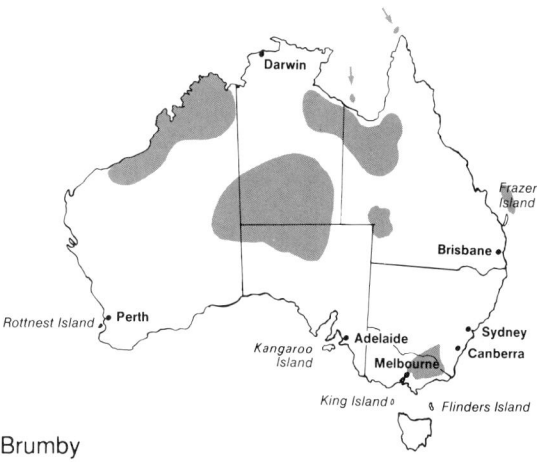

Brumby

remote areas of the Northern Territory, Western Australia and Queensland, as well as on some offshore islands.

The wild horses of the north-west and central Australia owe their small size, poor conformation and colour variation to the interbreeding that took place between the small horses introduced from Timor (Timor ponies) during the 1850s and the many domestic horses which escaped from breeding programmes set up to supply horses to the army for the overseas campaigns that Australians were engaged in at the time.

The beautiful mountain border country of Victoria and New South Wales is the home of our largest and soundest wild horses. Brumbies from here were immortalised by Banjo Paterson in his poem, 'The Man from Snowy River'. The wild horses do not look out of place in this vast and sparingly fenced region which takes in the mountain passes and open tussock tops of the Kosciusko Ranges, the high plains of Dargo, Omeo and Bogong with their many bush clad hills and the open grassy meadows dotted with stands of Woollybutts, Sassafras and twisted Snowgum trees. Place names such as Dead Horse Gap, Brumby Plain, Trap Yard Hill and many others show that wild horses have featured in the history of this region. During the Great Depression of the 1930s, the horses provided an income for those who chased them and then broke them to the saddle; others became involved in the horsemeat trade. Some were cruel men using piano-wire neck snares which they placed along the trails the brumbies habitually used. Those that did not die outright with broken necks, shared a fate similar to those who caught themselves in the trip-gate bushlog trap

yards. They experienced an agonising and lonely death due to starvation because many snares and traps were not checked often enough, particularly during the winter when there were heavy snow falls and blizzards.

Thankfully this cruelty has passed, allowing these small bands of bush horses to roam the border country relatively freely. Here the brumby is commonly seen in the lower altitude, timbered grassy flats during winter, seeking refuge from the snow and blizzards of the open high country. Brumbies live in small bands of usually one stallion and five or six mares. With the coming of spring, the pregnant mares seek out some quiet place in which to give birth to their foals. These are born mostly during the night, and can stand within an hour of being born, losing most of their wobbliness in a matter of hours. As the morning sun warms them it seems to put power into their muscles, for in no time at all they can run as fast as their mothers. As summer approaches and as the last of the snow melts, all manner of plants begin to burst with growth, encouraging the horses up to the high country to gorge themselves on the lush feed. The small groups of winter gather into large herds. This ensures a good mix of bloodlines.

As autumn draws near, the once timid and gangly foals grow into frisky and boisterous adolescents; their uneasy behaviour gradually spreads throughout the herd; the stallions begin to stir and become restless and domineering as the mating season approaches. They will begin to cut out breeding mares and to round them up into small bands, ready to run them off to the lowlands where they will once more spend the winter.

The wild stallions fight savagely to secure mares. This not only ensures nature's way of the fittest being the ones to breed, but also causes competition amongst members of the herd. Fighting disperses the herd so that it is unusual for stallions to have the opportunity to breed with their daughters of previous seasons, which would result in a weakening of the bloodlines.

The brumby stallion is no-one's pet. They should never be trusted as they show no fear of people, and when confronted will stand their ground and place themselves between those that challenge them and their mares, rather than back off. They snort and stamp their feet until the mares have made good their escape.

Donkey

The donkey was brought to Australia as a beast of burden at the time of the first settlements. Later, as the grazing lands were being opened up during the 1880s, very large numbers of them were imported to provide transport for a great variety of goods over different types of terrain.

The settlers' choice of the donkey was a good one, for this sturdy creature had been filling this role for centuries. The donkey can carry more weight for longer distances over the roughest of terrain, with less amount of fuss, than any other creature. They can obtain sufficient food where other animals would starve, and for short periods they can get by on the moisture obtained from the nightly dew on plants. With apparent ease they cope with the incredible heat and the freezing nights of the outback, the extremes of dust, sand and gibber of the inland, and the cold, wet mud and rocks of the coastal mountains. Little wonder the explorers chose them over other animals when searching for grazing lands for the sheep farmers, and

outward routes for heavy wool bales.

Donkeys were set to work at nearly every task on this new frontier: clearing land by plough, carrying posts and rails for fences, water carting, and carrying provisions and supplies for farmers, miners and graziers. They carried the raw materials in and carried out the riches.

In circumstances where the donkey lacked the physical strength for the task at hand, it was bred with the horse to produce the mule—an animal possessing the strength and size of the horse, whilst retaining the surefootedness, hardiness and quieter disposition of the donkey. Mules, however, are unable to breed.

Many donkeys escaped from these breeding programmes, or were simply let go when they were no longer required. Similarly, others gained their freedom or were abandoned due to the passage of time and coming of mechanisation and other modes of transport— they had simply outlived their usefulness.

Today there are hundreds of thousands of wild donkeys inhabiting the arid areas of Australia from the Kimberleys of Western Australia throughout the semi-deserts of South Australia, Northern Territory, Queensland, isolated areas of north-western New South Wales and into the Mallee of Victoria.

It is necessary to control the wild horses

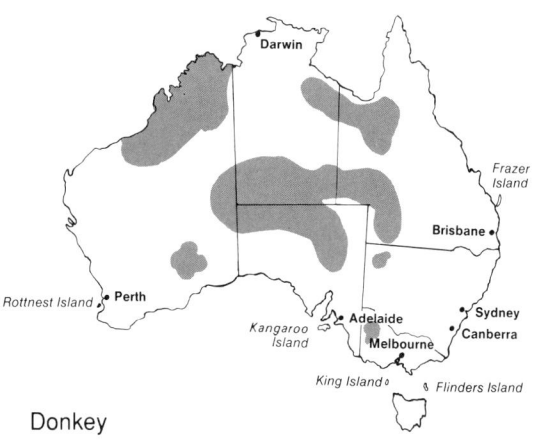

Donkey

and donkeys throughout the inland and northern Australia because they spread disease, compete with our grazing animals and damage the environment. Thousands are disposed of, equal numbers are shot for the pet food trade, whilst others are caught and processed in abattoirs for export to Japan and Europe, where horsemeat is a table delicacy and commands high prices. Others are caught and broken in, ensuring an uncomfortable ride for unsuspecting city buyers.

Camel

Camels were in Australia long before the famous Burke and Wills expedition in 1860, but they imported their own for their trek dubbed 'the Incredible Journey'. Camels gained popularity after this journey, and they were much in demand by those proposing expeditions into the interior during the 1870s, as they had heard accounts from other explorers of the suitability of these 'ships of the desert' and of the hardships they could withstand.

Whilst ordinary animals could not cope, the camel's legendary capacity for dealing with incredibly harsh conditions was well known. The camel is able to care for itself. This self-reliance was a valuable attribute on expeditions into the unknown. The camel's tough rubbery lips easily cope with needle-sharp thorns, woody desert spinifex and saltbush, sun-baked acacia leaves and other desert plants. There was no need to carry food for them; camels will maintain condition on shrubs and other vegetation that few animals would look at twice. However, the camel's great feature is its capacity to store moisture and keep a food reserve in its hump. More importantly, camels make these stored reserves last. Horses are not suited to the hard going of inland travel and require watering twice daily, whereas camels are able to obtain sufficient moisture from what is deposited on plants by the dew of cold desert nights. Amazingly, they only need to drink water every ten to twelve days, during which time they may cover huge distances, sometimes as much as three hundred and fifty kilometres.

The camel's contribution to the initial discovery of the vast inland grazing lands, and the access routes it later created, facilitated the rapid development that took place in these areas. Camels had proven themselves so suitable in this role that during the forty years between 1860 to 1900, farms were established to breed them. Many more were imported along with their Afghan and Pathan drivers to handle them. These colourful cameleers, each one in charge of a team of two dozen or more of these cantankerous creatures, were, it was said, as temperamental as the beasts they controlled. One needs great understanding and experience to obtain the best from a camel.

Long teams of camels assisted in the
cont'd on page 65

Above Once introduced the European goldfinch flourished on weeds, including thistles that had been accidentally introduced.

Below: Feral turkeys occur in considerable numbers on Flinders Island in Bass Strait. They originated from the stock of soldier settlers.

Above: Feral pigeons, perhaps the most common bird in the world, are found in towns, cities and wherever grain is stored.

Below: European carp can live out of water for a considerable time and so they were quite readily transported to inland areas.

Brown trout, on average, grow considerably larger in Australia than in Europe.

Prickly pear, has a pretty flower. It is reputed to have come to Australia with the first fleet.

Above: The fruit of the prickly pear is edible. In arid areas this cactus was used to hedge paddocks.

Below: Prickly pear infestation. It covered some twenty-four million hectares in the 1920s.

The water hyacinth has a pretty flower but it has proved to be a nuisance as it rapidly chokes lakes and waterways.

Above: Daffodils appear each year and they will probably continue to do so long after the mustering hut has disappeared.

Below: Dandelions have parachute-type seeds which facilitate their wide dispersal by wind.

55

Camel melons, which grow widely in the outback, where they were accidentally introduced by Afghans and their camels.

Above: St John's wort might look attractive but it became a pest; it is controlled by the introduced chrysomela beetle.

Below: Scotch thistles, like most other weeds, were probably accidentally introduced in the soils surrounding imported plants.

Above: Bathurst burr, it seems, was introduced from Chile, entangled in the tails of imported horses.

Below: As a single specimen, the stemless thistle is an attractive and unusual plant. It came from the Mediterranean.

Star thistles are one variety of prickly invaders of grazing land. Thistles are probably the most widespead of introduced plants.

A vine hawk moth on lantana, an introduced plant which escaped from settlers' gardens.

Above: The colourful larva of the vine moth.

Below: Cinnabar moth, introduced as a biological control agent for yellow flowered ragwort.

Cabbage moths are just one pest that would have been inadvertently introduced with their food source.

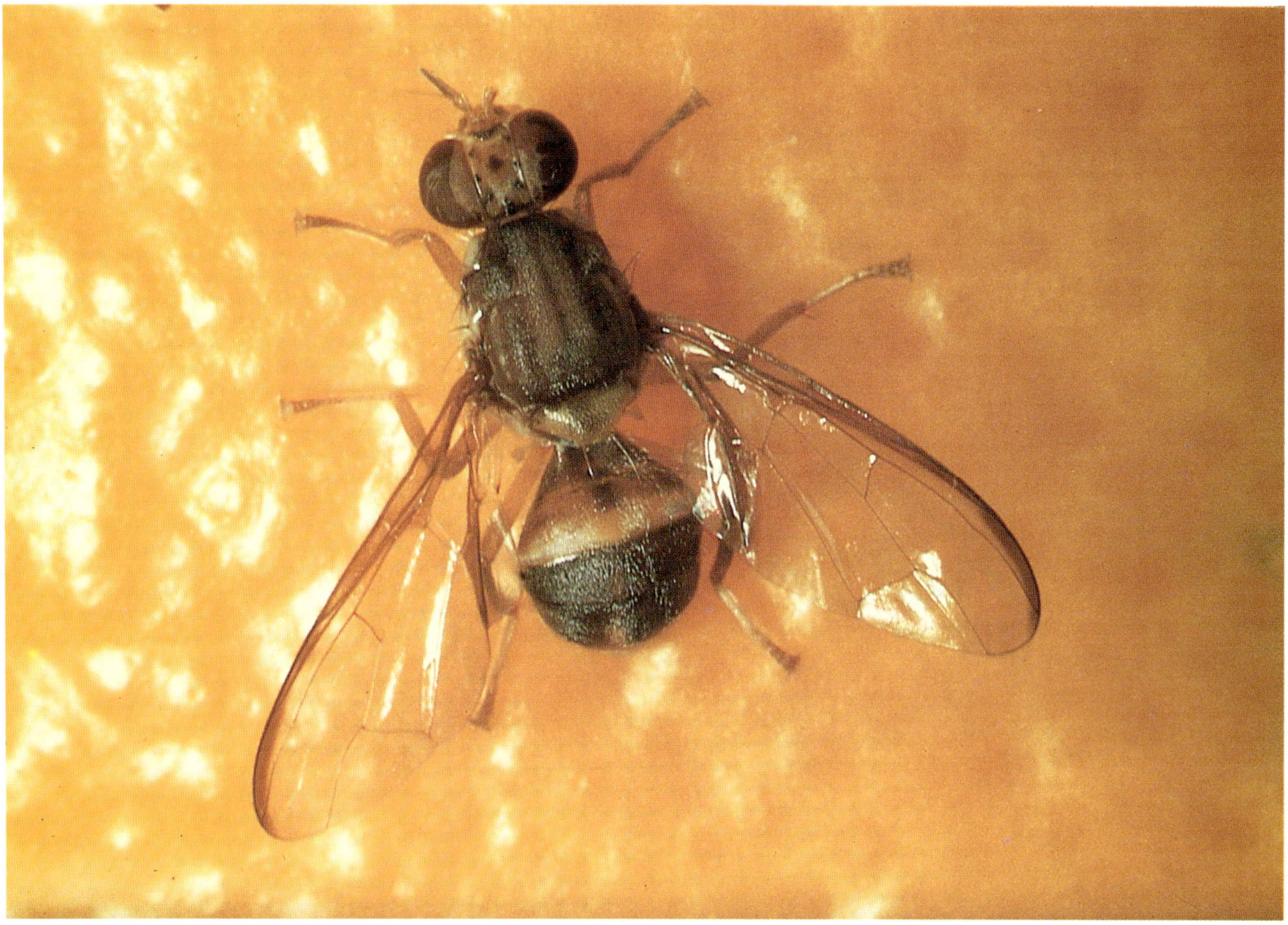

Above: Mediterranean fruit fly. The maggots hatch in fruit and so render it useless.

Below: The codling moth bores unerringly into the core of apples and rapidly spoils the fruit.

Above: White mealy bugs, another unwanted introduction, attacking a gladiolus bulb.

Below: The larvae of the Emperer gum moth, a native silkworm, readily feeds on the peppercorn tree.

building of the Trans-Continental Railway and the Overland Telegraph. They shifted the mountains of soil dug out to make huge dams and created miles of irrigation channels. Thousands of them were used for transport around the goldfields of Kalgoorlie in Western Australia. They hauled mail coaches, carted water and carried outback policemen on their patrols. They transported the materials needed to construct the lengthy rabbit fence along the borders of three states, and when this was later converted to the dingo fence, they were used by the men whose job it was to patrol and mend it.

Camels relish the conditions of heat, sand, rock strewn plains and salt encrusted wastes, places where other animals can't or won't go. Where heavy wagons broke up, or became hopelessly bogged, camels proved their efficiency and superiority in carrying most goods.

They were particularly valued for their transportation of wool from the booming grazing properties. Bales of wool are heavy (270 kg) and awkward things to handle; there is no feasible way to load them onto the back of a horse, donkey or mule. Most could not rise from the ground with this weight, let alone carry it for any distance. If working in teams, half of these animals would be needed to carry feed and water; quite apart from some apparatus to load and unload them when resting during the trek. Camels, on the other hand, can be conveniently loaded with a wool bale either side of their hump whilst they sit on the ground. They are able to rise to their feet under this enormous weight (540 kg) and then carry it very long distances, obtaining most of their food and water needs themselves along the way.

An estimated twenty thousand wild camels now roam throughout the regions where they were once used, in Central Australia, on the Nullarbor Plain and in the desert areas of South Australia, Queensland and the Northern Territory.

Australian camels have developed a hardy resistance to disease and are much in demand overseas for circuses. Some are even exported back to the countries they first came from. It is considered that they are not harmful to the environment here, although some landowners consider them pests on their properties and have to control them. Many were sold in the past not for their meat or skin, but for the fat of their hump. This was considered an excellent bait for dingoes, as it wouldn't dry out in the intense heat of the outback. It was laced with strychnine and dropped from a plane.

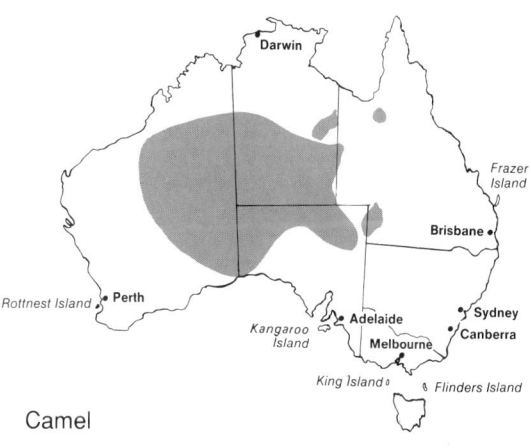

Camel

Water Buffalo

The domestic water buffalo of Asia and India was first introduced to Australia from Timor during the 1820s, to a military outpost on Melville Island north of Darwin.

The precise reason for the buffaloes' introduction is obscure, although they offer a superb means of transport through wet and muddy areas. However, they were not found to be of much use in Australia, and within two years of being introduced, they were set free in the bush. It wasn't long before numerous herds were seen, scattered kilometres from their release point.

The coastal plains of tropical northern Australia are subject to seasonal monsoonal rains which flood low-lying areas and create vast swamps and shallow lagoons. This so closely resembles the native habitat of the water buffalo that they quickly thrived.

Buffaloes are impressive animals. Their large grey and often mud-caked bodies are heavily muscled and they often attain weights of half a tonne. Their dangerous looking, wide flat horns assume massive proportions, sometimes approaching two metres across. The buffalo's threatening appearance, however, belies its true placid nature for it only becomes aggressive when cornered or severely annoyed.

Since the time of their introduction, buffalo numbers quickly built to over one hundred and fifty thousand. Enterprising settlers were quick to hunt them and establish industries using their meat for pet food, and their hides. Both meat and live animals have been exported back to Asia.

Water Buffalo

which are of concern to cattlemen. Authorities have introduced various species of dung beetles, in the hope of limiting the breeding of this fly.

Water buffalo, along with wild scrub cattle, feral pigs, donkeys and brumbies, are capable of spreading serious contagious diseases and so they interfere with the current disease eradication programme of tuberculosis and brucellosis from our cattle in the north. It is feared that animals such as the buffalo could be the means by which an accidental introduction of foot and mouth disease might be spread. Such infestation could cripple Australia's livestock export industry. For this reason, buffaloes are subject to a total elimination programme by the authorities in some areas. The aim is to create buffer zones to halt the spread of this disease, should it gain entry. All manner of means are being used to eliminate these animals from the wild: horseback round-ups, helicopter mustering and shooting programmes, and catching by special four-wheel drive vehicles. Farming of some of them, under strict controls, will supply the export industries that have been created.

Buffaloes are considered a problem by the pastoral industry in that they compete with stock for grazing, damage fences and muddy waterholes with their wallowing habits. They have had some deleterious effect on the nesting of the native magpie goose. With the buffalo came buffalo flies,

Other Wild Cattle

Wild banteng cattle, from Bali in Indonesia, are heavy bodied beasts, with short horns and a distinctive white patch on their rump. It is not known why they were brought in to Australia, although they would have suited the climate of the Top End where they were introduced to the same area as the water buffalo. It is estimated that there are only about one thousand of them, and it is most likely that they will be included in the disease eradication campaign. Some have found their way into breeding farms to be crossed with other breeds, in the hope that they will pass on their hardiness and size.

Wild zebu cattle were introduced from India to Queensland in 1910, where it was thought they may prove more suitable to the conditions than the earlier domesticated European breeds. These too are large animals with characteristic shoulder humps and masses of skin folds on their lower necks. They have been cross-bred with European cattle, as have many breeds from hot climates, and this has resulted in nearly all Queensland cattle possessing some signs of shoulder humps, skin folds and what appear to be almost hairless hides. Apart from their capacity to do better in tropical and semi-arid zones, the humped breeds show a high resistance to tick fever, although the ticks freely live on their bodies. In fact, it is claimed that an early introduction of zebu cattle (which were not destined for

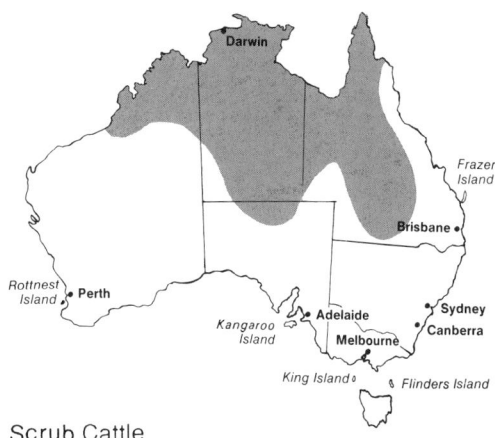
Scrub Cattle

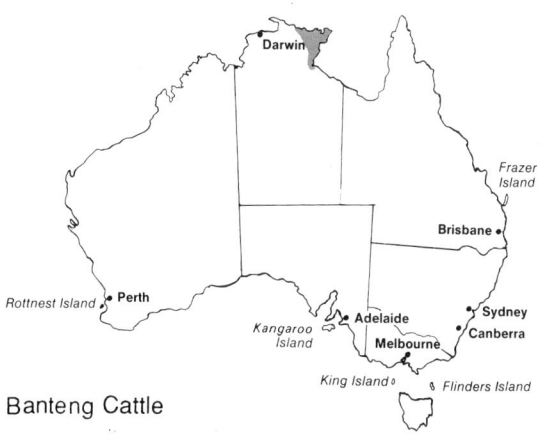
Banteng Cattle

release) was responsible for the accidental introduction of the cattle tick.

Wild scrub cattle cannot be described as truly feral for they only live in the wild because they have evaded capture. It is not intentional that they are free, but it would require too much expense and effort to round them all up. Many may have lived their whole life uncontrolled and, as a result, have become clever, difficult and dangerous to handle. They, too, are targetted in the overall disease control programme to rid areas of free-living feral animals.

Wild Pig

The common domestic pig first came to live in the wild in Australia after being deliberately released by many early explorers, including Captain James Cook. Other mariners, sealers and whalers also made releases into these newly-discovered lands and isolated islands. The pigs were intended to provide a ready source of meat for them should they return, or for those unfortunate enough to be shipwrecked, which was a common occurrence in the uncharted waters of those times.

Pigs also gained their freedom from the earliest times of settlement, either by being abandoned, or by simply escaping. They were allowed to roam freely in those days to obtain feed wherever they could and many simply wandered off.

We now have millions of feral pigs throughout Australia. They are found in every type of terrain, from the mountains to the coast. They are found throughout the monsoon belt of northern Australia and the great river systems of central New South Wales and Queensland, as well as on many islands off the coast.

Pigs in the wild have become extremely adaptable and interesting creatures but they are hardly attractive with their mud-caked bodies, bristling coarse hair and sharp protruding tusks.

The pig is better equipped than many other animals to survive the hardships of life in the wild. It is an omnivore, and so it is able to enjoy a wide variety of plant and animal foods. Its wide diet includes grass roots, earthworms, beetles, grasshoppers, frogs, fish, mice and the meat of carcasses of almost all animals. The pig also eats the

eggs of ground nesting birds, turtles and crocodiles. They will root out the burrows of rabbits, eating the young; they do the same in the burrows of the mutton-birds which nest on many islands of southern Australia. They often raid crops of all kinds, and will virtually plough up a paddock with their powerful snouts to upturn and expose the roots of grasses and other plants, the larvae of insects, and various fungi.

Graziers do not like wild pigs and wage a constant war against them, for the pigs seriously affect everything that is grown or sown. They also kill healthy lambs. Wild pigs are subjected to massive poisoning campaigns as well as every other means of control to reduce their numbers.

These pigs are widely hunted for sport, their dangerously curved tusks being considered the prize. Some hunters use their meat, although this habit is unwise, as the meat from wild pigs often contains diseases and varieties of tapeworms which are harmful to humans. Few lone hunters choose to stalk the pig in the watery maze of marshes and the dense lignum swamps that the pigs enjoy, for to come face to face with a full grown boar at close range is frightening. Many hunters prefer to use dogs to help them in the hunt. They go to considerable lengths to obtain suitable dogs and fit them with very wide and thick leather collars to avoid thrusts from the pig's razor sharp tusks. The dog not only needs a collar but it must be born with a natural ability to handle pigs. Wild pigs should never be underestimated; they will charge and chase aggressors, regardless of size, and they will fight savagely at close quarters inflicting shocking injuries to man and beast alike.

In recent times, a booming export market in wild pork meat has been developed, supplying this field-shot product to Germany. This lucrative industry for hundreds of thousands of wild pigs each year goes some way towards reducing their numbers. The authorities too, are now making serious efforts to totally eliminate them from certain areas as part of disease control programmes, and to control them in other areas. Wild pigs affect too many of our native animals, fish, birds and other creatures. For this reason alone, they need to be controlled. It seems that the wild pig is too adaptable for total elimination, however. In 1974, when Lake Eyre filled for the first time since European settlement in Australia, it was interesting to see that wild pigs had followed the flood waters down towards this lake from their previous known range limit, and now occupy country they had never been in before.

Wild Pig

Wild Goat

The goat is yet another domestic animal that now lives in the wild. Goats occur in every state in Australia, from throughout the vast semi-arid desert country to the hills and mountains close to our cities and towns.

It is estimated that there are now six million wild goats in Australia. Most have gained their freedom and bred up to these numbers for the same reasons as other feral animals. Goats, like pigs, were purposely released on islands even before settlement. The goat's inherent climbing agility has facilitated its escape from captivity. There have been many attempts in the past to establish mohair wool industries but these attempts most often failed and the goats were set free or abandoned.

Goats were kept on farms and in towns by many miners and prospectors. They not only provided meat and milk but were efficient scrub clearers as well. Some were used on farms to haul firewood, milk and water. Others provided personal transport for children and adults on trips to church, school and town. The small stout carts (the origin of the billycart), were pulled either by one goat, or teams, depending on the load.

Most country people have amusing stories to tell about wild goats. Longreach in central Queensland is a very hot and dry place which was once plagued by goats. Whilst it is normally common practice when in outback towns to park your car under the shade of trees, the locals would not dare do this as the goats invariably used the cars to climb up to the town's trees to get to the leaves. These inviting shady spots were reserved for unsuspecting 'out of towners' in the early days of motoring. Having parked their car, they would often return later to find

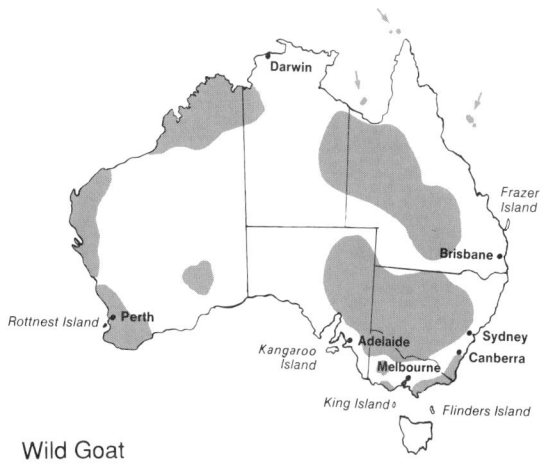

Wild Goat

that goats had fallen or jumped out of the trees and were left, legs dangling through the torn canvas hoods of the cars.

'Longreach Lamb' was a speciality dish of the locals, for any dish on the menu purportedly featuring lamb was invariably goat, sheep and lambs being too valuable for wool production to be killed for food.

In the flat and scrubby outback country the goats tend to rely heavily on their exceptional eyesight, particularly when forced by the oppressive heat to drink frequently at waterholes and bores. They must share these with birds, numerous kangaroos and in some areas pigs and occasionally dingoes as well. In such surroundings the goat's normal carefree attitude gives way to cautious alertness.

The lead nanny or billy of the herd stands on the scrub edge, apprehensively surveying the waterhole for danger. With each step forward it gains confidence until finally it bleats, giving the signal that the coast is clear. The herd then advances from the scrub in an almost instantaneous mad and jostling dash for the water. Once at the water's edge they will drink steadily regardless of the disturbance created by the birds and other animals. The billies are usually belligerent and not easily bullied by other animals, so it is odd to see them quickly give ground to an emu, especially when they have the ability to stand off the very best of dogs and are more than a match for a single dingo or wild pig.

Breeding takes place throughout the year, although most kids are born during the autumn months so that they are weaned as the flush of spring growth appears. Most nannies have twins, usually one male and one female, although three kids born at the one time are not uncommon. They are quaint little creatures that can be of almost any colour: black, white, grey, brown and all the shades in between. Very often their coat is a mixture of two or more colours.

The feral goat has possibly enjoyed the greatest amount of freedom of any animal in Australia simply because they are not the chosen food of any predator, neither are they considered good sport by most hunters (although both their long curved horns and multi-coloured skins are prized trophies to some). Indeed, it has only been in the last few years that there has been any interest at all shown in the wild goat and this is due to a resurgence of interest in the mohair and cashmere industries. Feral goat populations contain herds that are rich in these fibres and as the herds are free for the taking, it was quickly learned that money was to be made from them. Every year now, hundreds of thousands are rounded up not only to provide cheap foundation breeding stock for the growth of these valuable fibres but also for their thin hides which are eagerly sought by leather craftsmen overseas. The meat of the goat, or 'chevron' as it is called, is also valuable as it is still a basic meat in both Asia and the Middle East where it is much in demand. Export industries are constantly growing to service this trade.

Goats can have a dramatic damaging effect on native vegetation. Vast areas of Australia have been overgrazed to the point where they may never recover but goats cannot be blamed entirely for this. It is more frequently the fault of unmanaged sheep during the early days of settlement and later the damage caused by rabbits.

Feral Cat

The common domestic house cat is a favourite pet. Many live a life of luxury, lavished with expensive and often exotic foods. This doesn't stop their liking for night-time wandering during which they have total freedom to hunt for themselves and maintain their wild instincts.

The domestic cat retains an aloofness and a wild side to its nature and behaviour. We have not won from cats the obedience and submissiveness that we have won from dogs.

The feral cat is one that lives entirely in the wild, hunting its own foods. It is not a 'stray' nor is it an 'alley cat', of which there are many thousands.

Feral cats are found throughout Australia, in our driest deserts, in forests and mountains, coastal beaches, offshore islands and in the bushland close to our cities and towns. These cats now occur in very large numbers due to deliberate breeding campaigns in the days of the rabbit plagues. They were bred in thousands and taken everywhere the rabbit was thought to be. Even today some farmers still dump kittens in rabbit warrens to fend for themselves.

People from cities and towns dump thousands of unwanted cats in the bush each year. They have not the heart to take their lives themselves, and won't pay the fees to have it done. In Australia there are not the facilities available at local councils or shire level to dispose of them humanely, as is the practice in many countries overseas where the authorities recognise that domestic cats cannot be tied up and restricted to a yard like dogs. Cats usually come and go as they please which makes their breeding activities all the more difficult to control. The resultant births from these matings, an all too common occurrence, allows for the feral cat population to be added to daily.

Feral cats live in the wild at the expense of any native creature they can catch, and although some may live almost entirely on rabbits, it is not the general rule, as was previously thought. Native and introduced rats and mice are eaten, as well as possums, birds of every kind, lizards, frogs, snakes and indeed anything else they have a taste for. Cats are skillful predators and often grow very large in the wild, increasing their already formidable abilities.

Whilst they continue to be a direct and ongoing threat to our wildlife, they also spread diseases to sheep which can then be readily contracted by humans. It seems little can be done to control or eliminate them. Although there are diseases which could wipe them out, authorities are loathe to introduce them for they would probably affect domestic cats as well. Actions concerning people's pets are emotional ones and so they are not popular with governments.

The skins of feral cats have become quite valuable, sought after in recent years as a substitute for the pelts of the

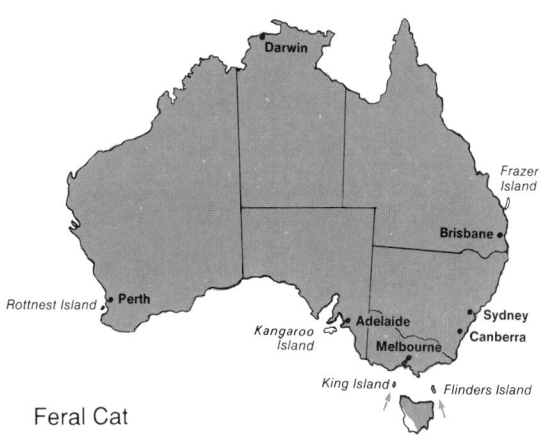

Feral Cat

threatened fur seal. Thousands of cat skins find their way to the city fur auctions, suggesting some reduction in their wild numbers is taking place. On the other hand, it seems, equal numbers of cats disappear, never returning to their city owners.

Feral Dog

The common domestic dog is another animal that now lives in the wild in many parts of Australia.

Feral dogs are most numerous in Victoria and New South Wales where they live in areas of the Great Dividing Range, particularly in bush hill country that adjoins sheep and cattle properties close to centres of human habitation. The feral dogs which are most frequently seen and trapped understandably show strong resemblance to those breeds which are commonly used as sheep and cattle working dogs in these areas. Over the years many farm dogs have wandered off from properties and never returned, some have become lost whilst mustering in thick bush, whilst others have been deliberately dumped, often as pups.

There are other feral dogs, particularly in parts of the dense forests of East Gippsland in Victoria, which have the appearance of hunting breeds. The elusive sambar deer, which occupy a vast area of this region, are frequently hunted with the assistance of packs of running hounds. Other large breeds of dog are used because they have the ability to bring a deer down, and hold it down. Doubtless many of these hunting dogs have become lost over the years in the excitement of the chase.

A large deer hound of this type was responsible for killing many sheep, lambs and calves in this locality. The damage was so extensive that it was first thought to have been caused by a black panther and rumours ran wild.

From time to time throughout many parts of Australia there are reported sightings of tigers, pumas, lions and other large cats running loose; however they are more likely to be a large breed of dog.

People from the major cities and towns are constantly and deliberately dumping litters of pups and adult dogs in country areas and in the bushland which fringes the areas where they live. Sometimes, well-intentioned gifts of cute pups grow into dogs that children and parents can not handle or don't want. Their owners often take them to country areas and simply let them go. There is certainly no place in the wild for the common domestic dog, for here they must kill for themselves and so they become full-time predators, inflicting damage on native wildlife as well as on farm stock. Feral dogs have a strong pack instinct and once formed in groups, cause more damage and take more lives than they need for food.

Unfortunately mountain dingoes, which are already few in number, share the same areas as the feral dog. The two readily interbreed, and this has caused them to all be classified as wild dogs in control operations to reduce their numbers.

Feral Dog

The mountain dingo will kill stock; however, recent research has shown that they much prefer native game. These dingoes only very rarely do the actual attacking and killing of stock although they will readily eat the remains of what is killed by cross-breds and feral dogs. Nevertheless, no distinction is made when trying to catch the culprits.

The alpine dingo is a magnificent, though largely misunderstood and mistreated animal. Whilst they cannot be excused for taking the stock they do, it would be interesting indeed to see what losses occurred if there were no feral dogs at all.

Dingo

The dingo deserves mention in this book, not only because of its relationship with domestic dogs that now live in the wild, but also because the dingo is often referred to as being an introduced animal, having been brought in by the Aboriginals some ten thousand years ago.

It could hardly be called a new wild animal considering the length of time it has been here. Yet Australians generally have not accepted it as being a native animal; it has never been regarded in the same way as the koala, kangaroo and emu. More than any other animal in Australia, the dingo is held in an unfortunate light, and is the subject of exaggerations, myths and legends. They are insatiable killers it is said, and although they are a species of dog, they are not readily subservient to people like other dogs. The dingo is aloof with a standoffish air and people are distrustful of this, for they don't like things they cannot control. We simply do not understand it, so rather than it being accepted as a native animal, we blame others for introducing it. Probably more money is spent on the control of this animal than on any other, except the rabbit.

We built a fence to keep them out of sheep country; the longest in the world, at some eight thousand, six hundred kilometres it was thousands of kilometres longer than the Great Wall of China.

We did all this, not knowing much about the animal at all. It took more than one hundred and fifty years of settlement, during which time a constant war was waged against the dingo, before anyone bothered to study this creature and sort out fact from fiction.

The Aborigines didn't attempt to domesticate them; they simply took advantage of the dingo's exceptional hunting abilities. They did not use them as we would use a hunting dog, by training and command. Rather, should they find a warrigal, as they called them, with a fresh kill, they would simply take it from them. The dingo would then most often follow them back to their camp and be fed sufficient food for it to remain with them. It was a repeated, loose arrangement, although pups were eagerly sought so as to provide a more dependent bonding. With the European settlement of Australia and its rapid expansion, particularly of the sheep grazing industry, dingoes took on a new importance. They were declared vermin, and graziers' Enemy No. 1. They were chased by hundreds of full-time trappers, and hundreds more part timers, who used traps, poisons and guns, indeed anything which would allow them to claim the bounty on the dingo's scalp. It was even suggested that dingoes be infected with fatal diseases such as distemper, and this would have been done except it was feared that farm and city dogs may be accidentally infected too.

To some dingoes, sheep may have been an instant attraction; however, to the majority it seems they would have been an acquired taste. Nevertheless the losses of sheep to these 'wild dogs' increased.

Dingoes had ample opportunity to acquire a taste for mutton. They probably first attacked the weaker of these 'new woolly animals' or began tasting the meat of already dead carcases (which incidentally they mostly prefer). They found that sheep were good to eat, and were relatively simple to catch and bring down, compared to native game. The latter became scarce as a result of the millions of sheep that took over their range.

Rabbits followed in the wake of the millions of sheep which were being pushed further into new areas to obtain feed. The sheep's close cropping made the vegetation ideal for the rabbit. This series of events was clearly evident in the semi-arid border country of New South Wales, South Australia and Queensland, a favoured natural range of the dingo, and an area where it has historically been most troublesome.

As the rabbit followed the sheep and bred in millions in country that was now made suitable for it, the dingoes experienced a population explosion. Rabbits provided them with an abundant, easily caught food supply and they also had millions of carcases to feed on, either from those that were caught in traps, or others that had died as a result of control operations.

Rabbits were becoming a huge problem and were threatening to move northwards from New South Wales and South Australia into Queensland. The Queensland government suggested to the New South Wales government that a fence should be built to halt their spread.

Other states eventually joined in this idea and so began the construction of the longest continuous netting fence in the world. Many previous rabbit fences were joined together and increased in height to provide a barrier for the dingo as well. The fence runs through some of the most desolate and isolated country in Australia. It runs across flat plains as far as the eye can see, before disappearing in mirages and shimmering heat haze. It zigzags through mulga and mallee scrub and up and over massive sand ridges, and sometimes disappears altogether under frequent sand storms. It even wanders across vast salt lakes where most animals would never venture. With the normal pattern of drought, which often lasts for years at a time in this region, feed for sheep ran out. Their stay here was a brief but devastating one; they had to be pulled out of the area and taken to grazing lands that could support them year round, albeit in much fewer numbers.

It is still commonly said that the only reason sheep cannot be grazed on the inland side of the fence is because of dingo attack. This is not so; the main reason is that the vegetation there is unable to sustain flocks of sheep of an economic size.

Cattle replaced sheep in this zone, primarily because they are not so hard on the vegetation; they don't crop it as closely as do sheep. Cattle also require far less handling than sheep, which need regular mustering for shearing, dipping, crutching and fly strike problems — this is an important economic consideration on these huge properties. Cattle, by their sheer size, are also less vulnerable to dingo attack.

One of the most interesting aspects concerning dingoes involved the Alsatian or German shepherd breed of dog. They were at first not numerous in Australia, and certainly not frequently found in sheep grazing areas here although, as their name suggests, they were commonly used for sheep mustering in their homeland. However, in 1929 this breed was unwelcome in Australia. It seems there were two reasons, one being the unfavourable feelings towards anything German at that time, and the other was that our pastoralists feared that this large dog bore too close a resemblance to the wolf. It was both bigger and stronger than the already troublesome dingo.

In any event, the graziers' prejudice was so strong against this breed that they were successful in bringing in legislation to ban the import of this breed from 1929 until 1972, a total of forty-three years!

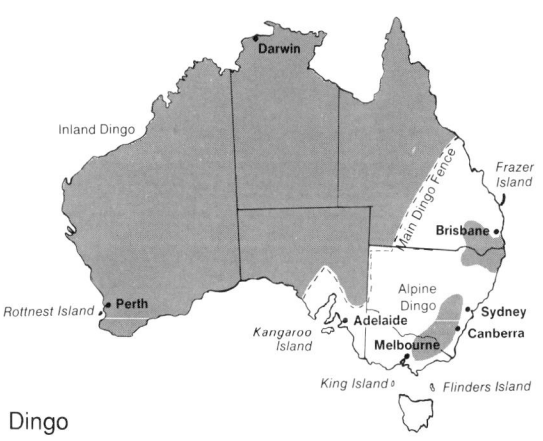

Dingo

So emotional were the graziers that they swayed the government with a successful mixture of scare tactics and an assumed superior knowledge of animal behaviour. They propounded the view to those in parliament that in all circumstances where the dingo and German shepherd dog should meet (and they may even purposely seek each other out), an instant love affair would transpire, producing a crossbred of frightening proportions and savagery.

Although there have been scientific studies undertaken to attempt to distinguish differences existing between dingoes, crossbreds and feral dogs, findings are inconclusive. So for all practical purposes, their differences in layman's judgement must remain those of appearance. Research did show that true dingoes have a somewhat different blood make-up which allows them to tolerate extreme heat and that they rarely, if ever, 'pant' as a domestic dog does after exertion. Their blood difference also affords them resistance to common fleas which live on domestic dogs and to native bush ticks, which attach themselves to domestic dogs with fatal results.

There are two distinct types of dingoes: those that inhabit the dry inland semi-desert country are generally of a light economical build, with a fine coat that is light yellow or almost white, particularly in summer; whereas the dingoes which inhabit the mountain forests and alpine areas of the Great Dividing Range from eastern Victoria through New South Wales and into south-east Queensland, are a heavier animal with a thick dense coat of reddish yellow. In both areas, coat colour darkens in winter and lightens in summer.

The dingo is for the most part a solitary animal and seems to lack the desire to move in a pack, although groups may be seen when there are shortages of game. It is a coming together more through circumstances than by organisation. However, in areas of human habitation they certainly form packs and it is then that they do the most damage. There is no question that in such areas the dingo has learned to be afraid of people and will use the cover and security of darkness— although they do not normally hunt at night—as well as the strength of numbers, to attack stock.

Groups of dingoes are most likely to be encountered during the mating season (March and April). Whilst the domestic dog is capable of producing two litters of pups per year, the dingo is capable of having only one. When matings occur between dingoes and domestic dogs, the dominant dingo characteristics are passed on so that most offspring of the first cross and following generations resemble true dingoes.

The female dingo, unlike the domestic dog, is also most choosey about her mate, and in most circumstances she will choose to mate each year with the same male. It seems they develop a bond with each other as they share the responsibility of raising the litter, which can comprise seven pups, rarely more, and of these not all will reach maturity. The bitch will not hesitate to kill any pups which show signs of weakness.

Observations show that dingoes most often hunt alone and usually only during early morning and late afternoon. Naturally, should one dingo have a kill that others witness, they expect to share the spoils. They are, above all else, opportunists as not every attempt at catching food is successful. Dingoes enjoy a very wide diet which includes ants, berries, fish, frogs, rodents, birds and their eggs, grasshoppers, snakes, lizards and virtually anything else they can catch. They will hunt kangaroos, wallabies, emus, and occasionally feral pigs and goats.

Sometimes they are seen chewing the dried bones of 'perishers' which are most often found on the edge of waterholes in the inland. Stockmen, when inspecting waterholes, often find sick or dying cattle close to water. They shoot them, as there is nothing that can be done for them, and they do not want them spreading disease or sickness to others. Dingoes obtain many meals by this practice.

In the rapidly fading light of evening, the dingoes greet one another in a most eager and friendly manner. They rub muzzles and wag tails just like domestic dogs do. In the areas of plentiful game each dingo beds down in a regular spot, not far from others, and fussily rearranges its bed in clean soft earth beside a shrub or bush. Dingoes do not bark, however they utter other sounds during the darkness of night. They snap and snarl, they cough and moan, and some yelp. They howl in their own distinctive way, not the mellow bay of a hound but an electric eerie call that once heard is never forgotten. They seem to use their howl as communication or for individual identification. Once bedded down they let others know of their location with an individual howl, and as one stops another starts. After each one has had its turn and it seems all are satisfied as to the whereabouts of others, no further sounds are heard from them throughout the night.

A Native Wild Dog Foundation has been formed by a concerned group to save the threatened alpine dingo. They trap them in the wild, breed from them, then foster them out to caring people. They walk them in public places and enter them in obedience trials, to show people their abilities and, ideally, convert people to their cause. Periodically they release them back to the wild, frustrating the authorities.

The dingo's scientific name is *Canis familiaris*, meaning familiar or common dog. Let us hope it is not necessary to change it to *Dingus rareus* for it would be unfortunate for them to become rare before the role they play in the wild of Australia is understood.

Controversy may haunt the dingo for many years to come; how differently we might have viewed them if they had never learned to like the meat of sheep.

BIRDS

On leaving the initial settlements, the pioneers and free settlers quickly began to spread out into the bushland of the new colony. There they began to see and hear more of the native bird life.

The ringing note of the bellbird was a common sound, yet the bird which made it was never easy to see. Parrots, cockatoos and rosellas of many beautiful colours swooped low through the trees; birds like these had only been known to Europeans from the jungles of exotic lands. The emu, which was seen in open country, was not unlike the ostrich of Africa. In the gullies and dense undergrowth of mountain valleys, the Australian ground thrush, a plump and tawny bird with a mottled chest, which resembled the thrush of England, could sometimes be seen.

One bird they would have seen was the lyrebird, gliding gracefully in front of them, its long and impressive tail flowing behind it. This bird, a marvellous mimic, caused them to assume that other settlers were nearby, for no matter how secluded and isolated the settler felt, he could hear sounds akin to the ringing of his axe, the rattling and clanging of his pots and pans, and even the barking of his dogs.

In the clearings of the eucalypt forests, the flame robin was often seen. Its breast was so brilliant that it far surpassed the colouring of the English robin redbreast, a bird fondly remembered by the immigrants. The kookaburra, sometimes called the laughing jackass, was seen and heard at dawn and dusk, and became known as the settlers' clock.

The new arrivals found a swan that was totally black, and had a voice. It could not have made a greater contrast with the mute white swan they had known in the old country.

So, amongst Australia's eight hundred or so different species of birds, there were some that reminded the settlers of home, and others that were so different from anything they had seen before or even imagined, that they must have listened and watched in wonder and amazement. This new land had an abundance of bird life, a richness and diversity of species unequalled in most countries, yet the colonists felt the need to add more.

The settlers laboured for many long years and overcame considerable hardship on the way to creating a self-sufficient colony. It was possibly only after this long period of enterprise that the settlers had time to reflect, to consider what their labours had created and what they still missed. The sight and song of the birds, what had become of them? Not all of them had disappeared; the willy wagtail could still be seen flitting after insects, the magpies' melodious song could still be heard, and both the white cockatoos and the pink and grey galahs were always ready to swoop down wherever grain crops were sown or reaped. But what became of the many other birds?

It was soon realised that the birds had gone with the bush; there was no habitat left for native birds. The land had been cleared and built on, there were more people and the resultant noise that accompanies them, there were new animals, new grasses, crops and plants. The trees and nesting sites of the birds were gone, the scrub was burnt and cleared and with it their food source. The birds had insufficient time to adapt to what was so rapidly being created.

Birds, possessing the freedom that flight

affords, can react quickly and move away from things they don't like or understand.

Whether the colonists were aware of the native birds' unwillingness or inability to accept this rapid change to their habitat is hard to say. The colonists wanted birds about them and what better than the birds they knew so well in their homeland? They so longed for the sounds and sights of these feathered creatures that they set about importing them and releasing them in Australia.

House Sparrow

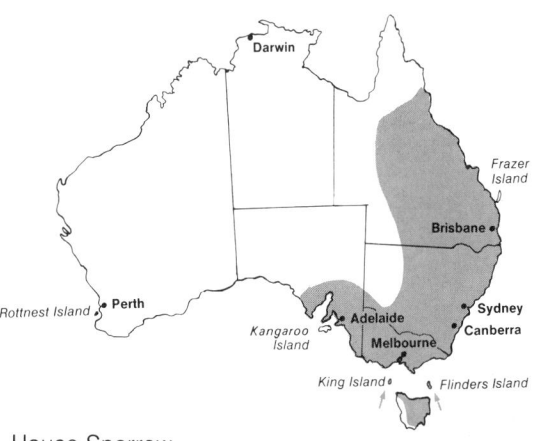

House Sparrow

The common European house sparrow was one of the first birds imported and released into the towns and settlements that had been vacated by the native birds. The sparrow was a natural choice. It has had such a long association with people in Europe that it could be said to be almost entirely domesticated. It does not live in the true wild state; it depends for food on crops, people's refuse and handouts.

Sparrows could have only been brought in for sentimental reasons. They have no song, unlike other birds, but instead an

incessant chattering and twittering. Their drab colouring, shape and small size, and their lack of any real flying ability, make them very ordinary but perhaps it is their commonness and their cheeky resourcefulness which are so attractive.

Whilst some sparrows feed in open paddocks seeking seeds and grain, and sometimes causing damage, the majority prefer the easier life of inhabiting granaries and storage silos, lazily swooping on what is spilled or left uncovered. In schoolyards you can set your watch by them, for no sooner is lunch-time over than they appear as if from nowhere, to enjoy leftovers from children's lunches.

When choosing a nest site the sparrow prefers to stay conveniently close to human habitation. It makes a crude nest of dry grass, bits of paper and thread and anything else it can scavenge and lines it with a bit of down and a few breast feathers.

Sparrows breed in both spring and summer, and more often if conditions are suitable. Their eggs only take fourteen days to hatch.

From the time that sparrows were first introduced to Australia, they have remained in the areas of the original settlements and towns, many of which have become large cities with sprawling suburbs. They have gone with us to country areas and will go wherever their little wings will carry them, throughout the areas of the milder climate of eastern Australia. They do not occur in Western Australia, the drier parts of the outback, or in central and northern Australia. They will not attempt long flights or subject themselves to hot areas, unless people provide their shade, their lodgings and most of their food.

Hedge Sparrow

Although this bird bears the name sparrow, and was released in the same areas as the house sparrow, it is quite a different bird. It is more retiring and lacks the cheek and resourcefulness of the house sparrow; it simply cannot compete on equal terms with it. Its shyness causes it to favour nesting in hedges and shrubs where its nest and eggs are similar to that of its relative. Although similar in size to the house sparrow, it is a more delicate bird with a slender, finely pointed beak, and is more of a chestnut colour than the dull brown of the house sparrow.

Hedge Sparrow

The distribution of the hedge sparrow (or tree sparrow as it is sometimes called) is said to include the vast area between Sydney and Melbourne, although it is doubtful if it as common as suggested. However, they are more accurately reported to be in good numbers in areas of the north-eastern Murray River valley, in both New South Wales and Victoria.

The hedge sparrow is primarily an insect eater and because of this habit and its choice of habitat, it is not dependent on people like the house sparrow. It does not damage crops, fruit and grain like its cousin.

Starling

The starling is another common town bird of Europe which was thought could fill the gap left by the withdrawal of the native birds from areas of settlement.

Should the native birds' retreat have been a slow one, this boisterous and aggressive foreigner would certainly have speeded it up, for the starling is a squabbler, even amongst its own kind. Their Latin name, *Sturnus vulgaris*, stern and vulgar, is most appropriate. They can get the better of most birds in competition for what food is available and they are messy in their nesting habits.

In cities and towns, starlings nest in the roofs of buildings. Nesting time for them seems to be a matter of urgency and impatience, for they hurriedly scavenge all manner of material, string, wool, paper, horsehair, straw and anything else they can find. Their nest is not sculpted into shape as most other birds' are, but is simply and crudely pushed together. Rather than line this tangled mess with soft down or feathers from their own breast, as is common with other birds, the starling uses the discarded feathers of other birds.

This gathering of materials can accumulate over many years and build up into massive piles in favoured nest sites of ceilings and eaves. This material is a fire hazard, and provides an ideal breeding ground for a mite which can inflict severe irritation on humans.

In country areas, starlings prefer to nest

Starling

in the hollows of trees just like most of our native birds. Being mild mannered in comparison to the starling, the native birds are forced to give way. The starling has a bullying habit of constructing its nest on top of another, whether it is occupied or not, by its own kind or any other. They are quarrelsome in brooding, and their nest sites can often be located simply by the sight of their smashed powder blue eggs on the ground below. These losses make no dent in their numbers, for they lay from four to eight eggs at a sitting and in the six to seven week breeding season of spring they often raise two or more families; little wonder that the starling is ever on the increase.

The starling is not a song bird. It makes a harsh rasping noise with clicking and whistling sounds coming from its vibrating throat and beak.

Although they appear to be black at a distance, on closer inspection, depending on the light, they exhibit a most beautiful metallic sheen of green, bronze and purple. Starlings, like most other birds, replace feathers as they become worn, and whilst this occurs during the moult, this bird changes its coat to one where distinctive buff and white speckles dot its plumage, giving it the look of an entirely different bird. When young, the starling is a different colour again, being a uniform shade of pale grey-brown.

The starling is more independent of humans than the house sparrow, possibly because of its more powerful flight, which allows it to range farther afield and, in some areas, live entirely on its own account.

Starlings like soft fruits and other produce, so that they sometimes cause considerable damage. On the other hand they assist us by eating troublesome insects. In open paddocks which have become flooded by rapidly rising rivers or heavy rain, forcing the insects from the soil, one often sees starlings in huge flocks, sometimes numbering thousands. At such times, the gregarious nature of starlings is evident. They are seldom seen individually but most often in a well-disciplined group, feeding, rising on the wing, wheeling, turning and descending to the ground as one. This close association is also apparent at dusk when they will gather in huge flocks to spend the night in a noisy communal roost. So many gather in the one spot that their droppings deface everything under them.

Starlings are most adaptable opportunists, encouraged by some who offer them nesting material and scorned by others who try everything to control them and prevent them from spreading to areas they do not already occupy.

The Western Australian authorities regard the starling as the aerial equivalent of the rabbit, and employ shooters and trappers in lonely areas of the Nullarbor Plain in South Australia to prevent their entry to their state.

Blackbird

The blackbird is considered one of the finest songsters of Europe and it was for this reason that it was introduced, even though those that proposed its release must have known full well its liking for the fruits of orchards and home gardens.

It is generally forgiven for the damage

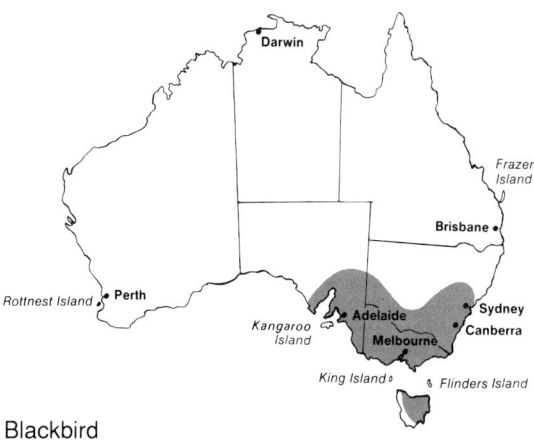

Blackbird

it causes because of the melodic warbling notes of its song, heard most frequently at dawn and dusk and during spring and summer showers.

The blackbird is relatively shy of people, even though it lives in suburban gardens. Its colouring is more suited to the forest or dark and shadowy areas and it will not feed in the open if it can get all of its needs under cover. When it does show itself in the open, we can see its intriguing method of obtaining worms from the soil. From a perch, blackbirds fly off in their characteristic low looping flight to alight on the ground somewhat heavily and proceed to skip and hop, disturbing the worms. Stopping suddenly, blackbirds will cock their heads first to one side then the other, in an effort to hear the telltale sounds of a worm wriggling in its tunnel. This method seems foolproof, for it is rare to see a blackbird without a worm in its beak after it has carried out this procedure.

Blackbirds are named from the male of the species, which is totally black bodied and has a yellow eye ring and yellow sharp-pointed bill. The female, which is similar in size, has a dark brown back and a mottled, streaked breast of grey-brown. They tend to be solitary, although pairs may be seen throughout the year. During the nesting period of spring and early summer the pair is inseparable, for they both share the duties of nest building and rearing of the young.

The nest of the blackbird is usually situated in thickly-leaved low shrubs and trees. It is a true construction; resembling a bowl in shape, it is made of intertwined dry grass, bark, twigs, leaves and rootlets, and it is consolidated at the base with mud or cow dung. It is lined with soft, fine grass into which are laid three to five blue-green eggs, densely speckled with reddish brown markings.

The conditions that suit the blackbird are those areas which are moist, with abundant greenery, particularly of introduced plants about suburban parks and gardens. They occur only in south-eastern Australia (including Tasmania), south of an imaginary line drawn roughly through Adelaide to Sydney, where they appear to be slowly increasing their range.

English people are sentimental about their birds, and have always held a high regard for the song of the blackbird. Shortly after its release in Australia in the 1860s, an early settler, hearing it for the first time after an absence of many years and thinking it to be a native bird, is said to have remarked: 'That bird has a lovely song, but not as good as the blackbird back home.'

Song Thrush

The song thrush is a close relative of the blackbird, sharing habits so similar that it is said that 'the blackbird is but a thrush, in a coat of ebony.' The thrush was introduced for the same reason as the blackbird. It is equal or even superior to its relative in song.

Similar in size, both male and female are graceful birds. They have olive-brown colouring, with a breast of light fawn with

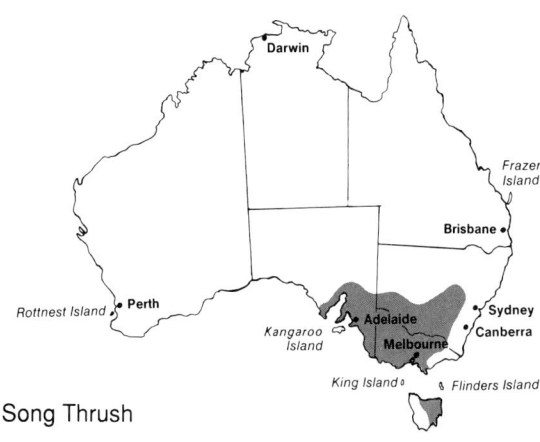

Song Thrush

dark brown speckles. Their diet includes insects and their larvae, moths, beetles and spiders, as well as all kinds of berries and small fruits but it does not show a liking for commercial orchard fruits like the blackbird does.

The thrush shares with the blackbird the special skill in catching earthworms. It is more readily observed as it is not so timid. However, this songster has a particular skill all of its own, and that is the way in which it removes the hard shell of the common introduced garden snail. The bill of the thrush is hardly strong enough to crush these awkward structures, so in order to remove the tender creature, it picks up the shell in its beak and strikes it on a flat stone or rock until the shell is cracked. Such rocks or stones are appropriately called 'the thrush's anvil'.

The thrush loves these molluscs which form a large part of its diet, and live snails were transported and released with the thrush to provide it with the tasty morsels it had long enjoyed at home. The garden snail was not only brought in with the thrush, but also came here uninvited, hiding amongst eagerly awaited imported plants. Snails, and there are many types, have since become such a common garden pest that a variety of chemicals have been devised to rid our gardens of them. These have not worked in reducing the overall numbers of snails, but have seriously reduced the numbers of the thrush. Whilst the thrush does not eat the chemical pellets or powders, it consumes vast numbers of snails which have absorbed these deadly poisons.

The nesting period of the thrush is a long one. Its melodious mating song can first be heard during courtship in autumn and lasts through to late spring and early summer. During this time they will lay several clutches of four bluish green eggs, spotted with black and greyish brown, in nests most often found in hedges, shrubs and other low-growing bushy plants. They have finely constructed cup-shaped nests made from grasses, mosses, twigs and rootlets. They are lined with mud, which is carefully smoothed then allowed to dry.

Many people living in Melbourne's suburbs, the thrushes' main range, resist using chemicals to control the damage snails cause, wishing to preserve this bird because the song of the thrush begs to be listened to.

English Skylark

The English skylark has been revered by poets for centuries, and this little bird's exhilarating song has been described as 'the very sunshine singing'. Little wonder the new settlers had pleasant memories of the skylark and considered it a valued introduction in the 1860s.

However, in Australia we already had two larks of our own: the singing bushlark and the ground lark or pipit. Both are so similar to the English skylark in appearance, song, flight and habits, that when any of them are encountered in the field they are all simply called the skylark. Their resemblance is so close that it would take an expert to distinguish one from another. Even highly regarded books confuse the flight patterns and eggs of one with another.

They are all similar in size and general appearance. The upper parts of their bodies are pale brown with black stripes on the feathers, the throat, breast and under parts are white. They breed throughout late spring and autumn in open grassy fields, building their cup-shaped nests on the ground. Nests usually contain four eggs. The English skylark's eggs are olive-brown and greyish in colour, whilst the eggs of both native birds are white with spots and blotches of dark brown.

The larks have similar flight patterns, whereby they rise vertically from the ground directly above their nest site, in an initial upward thrust. The English skylarks, by means of ever increasing upward spirals, rise to great heights so that they are almost invisible, whereupon they will begin to sing, sometimes for as long as five minutes or more. The native birds do not spiral but climb straight up, singing as they go, and do not reach the heights obtained by the English bird. All descend in much the same manner; they seem to drop straight down, then abruptly halt and hover, and they repeat this action, descending in stages. On nearing the ground they sometimes fly at grass height for a short distance, or alternatively alight on the ground and run some distance to the nest; rarely do any of the larks alight directly on the nest. The English skylark and our bushlark tend to walk on the ground whereas the native ground lark, or pipit, is often seen running in short bursts, its tail bobbing up and down at each stop.

These larks all prefer the habitat of open grasslands, which is in abundance in Australia, as are their preferred foods,

English Skylark

insects, grass seeds and shoots. So rather than competing with our native larks, it could be said that the native skylark competes with the English skylark, so common and numerous are the fields of European grasses and foreign insects found here. In summer the open fields from Adelaide through Victoria and New South Wales are enriched by the song of the skylark.

Indian Mynah

Originally this bird came from the steamy jungles of south-east Asia, hence its other name, the jungle mynah. This most adaptable of birds was also a companion of wild cattle, wild buffalo, many species of deer and the once common Indian rhinoceros in the clearings of the forest where these animals preferred to graze.

The intelligent mynah learnt long ago that an easy meal was to be had by perching on the backs of these animals and relieving them of annoying insects. This bond of cooperation and trust which developed between grazing animal and bird afforded the mynah another feeding opportunity. As the grazing animal feeds in the grass, its head movement and the warm breath from its nostrils disturbs the ground insects. The mynah takes full advantage of this, hopping about the ground close to the animal's head.

A demonstration of the mynah's intelligence and adaptability is that, in Australia, they have spread along the main roads and highways. Here instead of wild creatures disturbing the insects in the grass, the mynahs have learnt that passing motor vehicles create a wind disturbance which causes the insects in the roadside grass to move and give their presence away, allowing them to become easy prey. The birds also enjoy the food scraps they find on the roadside.

In the cities and towns, however, mynahs take any opportunity to scavenge in the streets, parks, and residential gardens for scraps of food. They also like seedlings and soft fruits.

Usually mynahs are found in pairs or in small groups of six or so. They have a distinctive hop as a means of getting around and an arrogant strut when walking. They tend to fly only short distances.

They are a rich dark tan in colour, have a black head and neck, and yellow bill, legs and eye patch. Their wings are not pointed at the tip as most birds' wings are, but are very rounded, with large white areas on the under surface; the tail is white tipped.

They are not a bird of song but make a sort of clattering whistle. They share communal roosts where they form a noisy and untidy mob.

Mynahs have shown a strong preference

Indian Mynah

for areas of human habitation. They seem reluctant to fly long distances which means they are unlikely to spread to new areas of their own accord, so they were deliberately introduced to many more areas than were other birds. Since their release in the 1860s they have remained in the main centres of human population, from Adelaide and along the eastern coastal belt to Brisbane. They also occur in the sugar cane growing area of north Queensland, where they were deliberately and repeatedly introduced to assist in the control of cane beetles and other insects. They had only limited success in this role, however, as they usually gravitated to populated areas where food was more easy to come by.

European Goldfinch

The European goldfinch is considered by many to be one of the most attractive of the birds introduced to our cities and towns. This pretty little bird has a mixture of gold, black and white striped wings with a brilliant crimson head and is about the size of the sparrow. Goldfinches found the early settlements much to their liking, particularly when the introduced weeds and thistles began to spread throughout the colony, for it is these plants which give them their other name, the 'thistle bird of Europe'.

The many varieties of thistles provide this bird with its major food source of seeds, although the goldfinch also enjoys feeding on small flying insects. The thistles also provide this bird with its nest building materials; the soft down of these plants forms the inner lining of their small cup-shaped nests, which are most often found in dense-leaved trees or shrubs of introduced species. The outer layer of the nest is made from long strands of dry grass wound and intertwined and sometimes bound with horsehair, wool and mosses. Usually three to four white eggs with rust-coloured flecks are laid in this cosy nest, although most often only two young are raised.

When it is their time to breed, they construct a nest which is identical to the one in which they were born. One can inspect goldfinch nests and find that they are all replicas of each other, a remarkable example of the strong hereditary traits birds possess, since young birds are not actually shown how to make a nest by their parents.

Nests of the goldfinches are often raided by canary fanciers who take young males to crossbreed with female canaries. The resultant offspring are unable to breed, but they have a singing voice which is unsurpassed.

The goldfinch lives on the fringes of most of our capital cities, from Perth to Brisbane, where it frequents paddocks or grasslands as well as suburban areas and gardens. It is most often seen in small groups aptly termed 'charms' or, during the non-breeding season, in flocks sometimes numbering hundreds. When goldfinches are all on the wing they give a delightful display of shimmering gold.

European Greenfinch

The European greenfinch is a close relative of the goldfinch. It is a little larger and a dull olive-green colour, with a yellowish breast and wing bars. Both birds were introduced during the 1860s into the same areas but the greenfinch has not become as numerous as its cousin. Whilst the goldfinch prefers the seeds found in the open grasslands, the

Red-whiskered Bulbul

European Greenfinch

greenfinch, from the shaded forests of Europe, has a larger beak which can easily handle the larger seeds such trees produce.

It seems that the relatively small population of greenfinches may be due, in part, to the fact that introduced European trees were not well established in Australia at the time the birds were released and thus they were not afforded an entirely suitable habitat nor their preferred food.

As the greenfinch prefers to live in the more dense and dark exotic wooded areas, it is not very frequently seen.

Red-whiskered Bulbul

This bird has the appearance of a woodpecker, with its pointed black upright crest. It was introduced in the same period and into the same localities as both the finches. Originally it failed to establish itself and many later attempts were made to introduce it, particularly to areas around Sydney where now it is apparently doing very well.

It is a member of a large family of similar birds from Asia and there is strong evidence that this bulbul, or some of its relatives, may occur in Melbourne and Adelaide and other large centres as well.

The red-whiskered bulbul is quite a common cage bird in Asia, although its noisy and monotonous song has caused many owners to set it free. It has long been accustomed to the company of people, and it readily accepts the habitat of parks and gardens in cities.

The bulbul is a colourful bird; it has a black head and neck, a dull brown body, a red splotch about the ear and white cheeks and underparts. This bird loves dense foliage. It obtains its nest materials such as twigs and other vegetable matter from its close surroundings. It lays up to four white eggs which are spotted with reddish brown.

The red-whiskered bulbul is insectivorous by nature, but it often causes some damage to flowers and fruits in its aggressive search for food, so it is not welcomed by gardeners.

Mute or White Swan

This beautiful bird is the royal bird of England. The white swans come under the

direct control of the Queen, who has delegated the responsibility for their welfare to a person who has the grand title of 'The Royal Keeper of the Swans'.

Although this elegant and graceful bird is found throughout most of Europe and parts of Asia, it is strongly associated with Britain and as our first immigrants were largely from England, it is not surprising that for sentimental reasons they wanted them introduced here. What better bird to remind the settlers of home?

Australia offered a black swan (the only black swan in the world), a bird of equal grace and beauty with a melodious call as well, but they were wild, and swam away or flew off when approached. The white swan was semi-domesticated, living in ornamental ponds, and rather than shunning people they eagerly awaited their handouts and so stayed in range to be admired.

Named the mute swan because of its lack of a call or song, white swans nevertheless make a variety of sounds, from various whistles and snorts, to aggressive hisses, when alarmed. When in flight, they can alter the pattern of their wing beat which creates minute differences in sound, allowing them to communicate with each other.

There is no accurate information available to tell us to which areas they were first introduced in Australia, but it has been suggested that they were probably tried in all capital cities and many provincial towns. Today there appears to be only two remaining colonies, one at Northam, north of Perth in Western Australia, and another at Lake Leake in northern Tasmania where their numbers are declining. In both areas they show no inclination to colonise in the wild. This might in part be due to their habit of only ranging within twenty kilometres of where they were born. In the past, quite surprisingly, they were not introduced to wild waterfowl areas for fear that they might oust the black swan, a fear which was unfounded as they co-exist very well.

Indian Spotted and Senegal Turtle Dove

Australia has many native species of doves and members of the pigeon family which are found in all types of natural habitat, yet the acclimatisation societies were strongly determined to introduce more. They began in the 1860s by introducing various Asian species, of which the spotted turtle dove is one, and fifty years later they were still importing and distributing this bird and its relation, the Senegal turtle dove.

The Senegal turtle dove was released in Perth, where it has become common, and it occurs in other centres of the south-west of the state. The spotted turtle dove and other Asian members of its family, with which it has subsequently interbred, were released in many areas from north Queensland to Perth, and in most large cities and towns in between, where they later became numerous.

The native pigeons and doves prefer a natural habitat whereas the imported doves are city birds, a heritage they acquired over centuries of living in crowded Asian countries. Both species are

Mute or White Swan

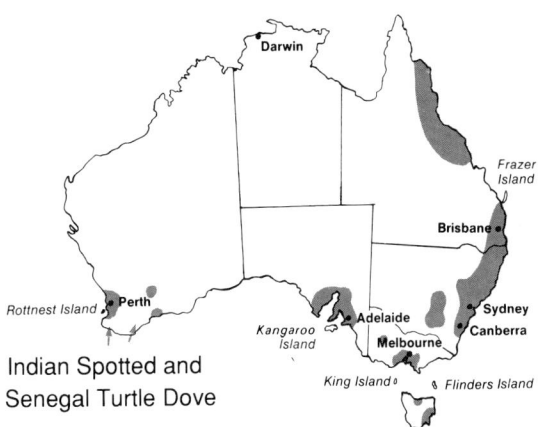

Indian Spotted and Senegal Turtle Dove

ground feeders and exist chiefly on grains that are stored or spilled during transportation through urban areas. They also obtain seeds from garden plants, and food scraps that can be found in parks and gardens and other open spaces in most cities and towns. In the country areas bordering towns and cities, they obtain seeds from more natural sources, although seeds from grain crops form a large part of their diet.

Like all doves and pigeons they both have rapid flight with clapping wing beats, although they alternate between rapid straight ahead flight and gliding. During courtship display they are seen to rise high in the air and on attaining a considerable height, they fold their wings close to their body and simply plummet towards earth at breath-taking speed and then pull out of this dive at the last moment and glide to a suitable perch. On landing, the males puff up their chest and throat, and with much bobbing and cooing attempt to impress their mate.

Their nest, containing one or two white eggs, is usually a platform of thin loose twigs and grass, hastily put together in almost any type of tree or shrub.

Indian Peafowl

We like to call this bird the peacock in Australia, for it is the male that is so attractive, with a glossy, almost iridescent sheen to its blue-green plumage and its magnificent shivering fan-shaped tail. It must surely be one of the most beautiful birds in the world.

Peafowls were primarily introduced for decoration, to be appealing in a semi-domesticated state, and they were not intended for release into the wild although a colony exists on Rottnest Island, off the Western Australian coast near Perth. The origin and reasons for this release or liberation are unknown.

Indian Peafowl

The Indian peafowl was intended to grace the city and town parks and give a civilised and cultured look to the manicured lawns of the grand homesteads which were built on European lines.

Although this bird's beauty cannot be denied, it seems perhaps too pretty and ostentatious for the Australian landscape. Its piercing call carries great distances.

Some people continue to raise this bird commercially, either to supply those that still seek it for decorative purposes, or to produce the valuable tail feathers from the males, of which ninety or so drop each year. Other peafowls appear on menus for those with exotic tastes.

Cattle Egret

The cattle egret got its name from its close association with the herbivores, such as buffaloes, antelope and wild species of cattle, with which it is usually seen walking and feeding.

They enjoy eating grasshoppers, and other insects that live in grasslands and

they particularly like the insects which are skin parasites on grazing animals. Cattle egrets are sometimes seen perched on the backs of these animals where they are readily tolerated because they bring relief by removing the annoying insects. The cattle egret was introduced into the Kimberley region of Western Australia in the 1950s to combat the cattle tick. The cattle tick, an accidental introduction, causes fever in cattle which makes them lose condition, and they often die as a result of heavy infestation. The cattle tick can spread through entire herds causing serious losses, with all the animals in the herd taking on the appearance of 'poor doers'. Ever since cattle were first grazed in the tropics, from the Kimberleys, across the Top End and down to the coastal areas of northern New South Wales, the cattle tick has been a problem. Whilst there is abundant grazing available in this vast region, the economic viability of the industry was largely dependent on control of the cattle tick, so it was thought the introduction of the cattle egret might be the answer.

However, the cattlemen did not realise that the egrets could not alone hope to cope with the ticks and the problems they caused. The blood-sucking parasites found the soft hides of British breeds of cattle easy to penetrate. Cattle from Asia, the tick's natural host, have evolved to be largely immune to their effect and so they can tolerate them and not lose condition in the way British breeds do. The cattle egret is increasingly common in the Top End, particularly in Queensland. There have also been reports of cattle egrets extending their range to the southern states, although when migrating they can be easily confused with native white egrets.

In the breeding season the cattle egret changes from its non-breeding white colouring to one with orange feathers on throat, head and back. The beak, feet and legs also change from yellow to a reddish-brown.

The nest usually consists of a platform of sticks and twigs, and normally contains three or four eggs with a blue-green tinge. The egrets share the waterways and nest sites with many native waterbirds in colonies which contain herons, spoonbills, ibis and cranes. This new arrival seems to enjoy an amicable relationship with native residents.

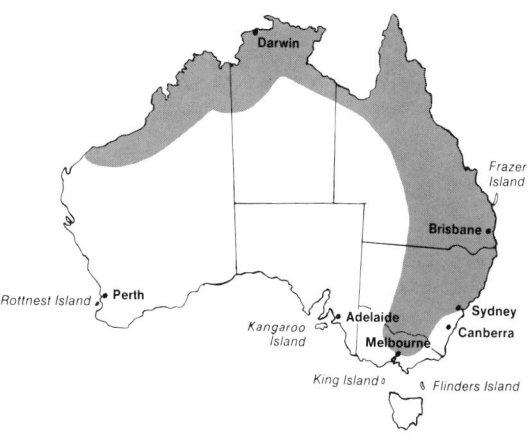

Cattle Egret

Ringneck Pheasant

Birds were not only imported expressly to remind the settlers of home, either by their colourful presence or familiar song, but were also imported specifically for sport.

It was not that Australia lacked sporting birds of its own, for old records show that enterprising shooters provided the colonies' markets with large quantities of quail, duck, bronzewing and other pigeons and bush turkeys. These native birds were found in great abundance and, more importantly, within easy reach of the main settlements, so that these professional hunters earned a very good living.

However, the sporting gentlemen of that era longed for traditional sport from the traditional game birds of Europe and the ringneck pheasant topped their list. These magnificently plumed birds were first introduced in the late 1800s, but their success at adapting to the new surroundings was dependent on their being able to escape from the impatient guns of those that introduced them, for no sooner did pheasant numbers build up in nursery hatcheries than they were released to face a barrage of shot. Those that did escape this onslaught found life in the wild Australian bush hard.

Many other releases of pheasants protected from shooting took place, however these too were mostly unsuccessful. Of all the releases that were made, the ringneck pheasant has only survived in any considerable number in two areas, Rottnest Island off the Western Australian coast near Perth and on King Island in Bass Strait.

Although there are reports of them in various places on the Australian mainland, these generally are not self-sustaining wild populations, but are more likely to be releases of caged or raised birds. Hunters have held the sporting qualities of this bird in such high esteem that, from the very earliest times of introduction here, they have been continually raising and releasing them in the hope of regular sport.

It is difficult to understand why this bird has failed to establish itself and come to terms with living in the wild in Australia, although it must be realised that pheasants in their native range and habitat do not exist in dense populations. They only provide sport for a large number of guns when they are artificially reared and set free, as is the case with the organised shoots that occur in England, Europe, America and New Zealand.

Chukar Partridge and California Quail

The chukar partridge and the California quail are two North American game birds that were introduced at about the same time as the ringneck pheasant to provide sport.

The chukar partridge is a plump and mottled feathered bird, a real speedster of the air which surrounds the high, semi-arid canyons and steep rocky slopes of the USA where it is considered by all who hunt it to be a premier game bird.

It is doubtful whether any of the first releases here enabled a continuing wild population to become established, for the birds were subjected to heavy hunting pressure almost as soon as they were

Ringneck Pheasant

released. It also seems doubtful that we provided a habitat which in any way resembled their native home, although there have been recent reports that new releases of chukar partridges are taking place in rocky mountainous country in New South Wales. This bird's future in the wild will largely depend on how closely our conditions meet its known requirements regarding food, shelter, climate and all of the other variables that go to make up this particular species' preferred habitat.

The California quail is another sporting

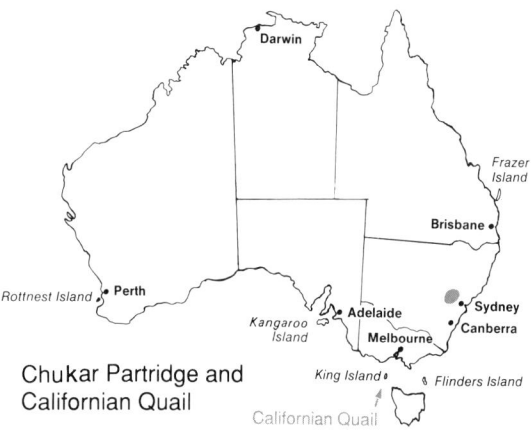

Chukar Partridge and Californian Quail

bird which makes characteristic 'explosions' from cover with clattering, rapid wing beat. It was most probably introduced, apart from providing another bird to hunt, because it is bigger than native quail. A hunter with a family of four would probably need to shoot a dozen or more of the natives to make a decent meal whereas three or four California quail would suffice.

This game bird still exists in reasonable numbers on King Island in Bass Strait; a much later release than those that occurred on the mainland, it is an area where they enjoy some protection from hunters as there are enforced closed seasons.

It seems certain that these birds will be regularly reintroduced in any terrain that is both suitable for the birds and convenient for the hunters who release them. Because of this, continuing isolated reports of these birds being sighted in the wild, are most likely to be accurate.

Mallard Duck

The mallard can almost fit into the category of a sporting bird, for although it is semi-domesticated, and the forebear of most domestic ducks, it is now found in its largest numbers in the wild.

The main purpose in releasing the mallard in Australia was to decorate the ponds of city parks and urban waterways, a role it had long enjoyed in Europe. Many were kept as a source of poultry meat by farmers and others, and they were usually allowed to roam free rather than be caged.

The mallard is very closely related to the native black duck and problems have arisen between the two. They share preferences for particular types of food and habitat, but more importantly they

Mallard Duck

interbreed, and herein lies the concern, as they very often share the same areas.

Amongst their own kind, there are more mallard males than females, and as she does the choosing, it leaves many males without a mate. However, when amongst populations of black ducks, the mallard drakes eagerly and more successfully compete with male blacks for female blacks. In the resulting crossbreeding, the mallard's characteristics are dominant; and there is a grave fear in Australia that it may seriously threaten the numbers of pure black ducks, as has already happened in New Zealand.

However, whilst the mallard is capable of migratory flights of two and a half thousand kilometres (sometimes covering three hundred and fifty kilometres in a day and attaining speeds of seventy kilometres per hour), a feat matched by the black duck, it is doubtful whether the mallards have any desire to cope with the harsh Australian outback conditions that are part of the normal migratory areas of the black duck. Mallards much prefer the easy life to be had near the main centres of human habitation.

Feral Pigeon

The feral pigeon is considered to be the most common bird in the world as it is found in almost all countries, both in rural areas, particularly where grain crops are grown, and in cities and towns where it feeds on handouts and discarded scraps. Feral pigeons are also found in large numbers around wharves, grain silos, railway yards and wherever grain is likely to be available either from storage or spillage.

The common pigeon is a descendant of the European rock dove, and the pigeons of today that show blue-grey colouring and iridescent mauve-green necks most resemble their wild ancestors of long ago, but feral pigeons can be of various colouring.

Feral pigeons maintain the same breeding habits as their ancient forebears in that they usually lay their two white eggs on ledges, whether they be on buildings, roofs, beams, rock ledges or cliffs. The nest, if it can be described as one, is usually just enough sticks or dry grass to prevent the eggs from rolling from the precarious positions on which the nest is placed. Because of their choice of nest sites and their prolific breeding abilities (nesting several times per year), feral pigeons have become quite a problem in cities, where they deface buildings with their droppings and cause blockages and water damage when their nest materials build up in drainage systems and roofs. The authorities have even resorted to placing realistic looking plastic snakes on the ledges of buildings in an effort to frighten the pigeons and deter them from landing.

Another cause for concern is that pigeons carry two diseases which are fatal to humans. Although it is not without risk, millions of people worldwide choose to keep these birds as a recreational interest, and gain much pleasure from marvelling at their legendary homing instincts and aerial feats. In fact, the pigeon is one of the few birds that people can have as a pet and yet allow complete freedom of flight;

Feral Pigeon

and it is from this freedom that feral populations arise.

The feral pigeon's impact on Australia is difficult to gauge because of the bird's uniqueness; it seems dependent on people in the cities, yet it can satisfactorily fend for itself in rural areas. It is even more difficult to know with any certainty which pigeons are truly feral, for their numbers are so great, they are so widespread, and their appearance and colouring are so diverse because of the amount of cross-breeding. They are heavily preyed upon by native hawks and falcons but unfortunately these predatory birds are shot on sight by those that have an interest in pigeons.

Ostrich

The ostrich was brought to Australia to be farmed for the production of its feathers which were in great demand by the fashion industry both here and overseas. At its height, in the late 1800s and early 1900s, it was a very large and lucrative industry.

Africa, the native home of this bird, was the world's principal supplier to the fashion market. The ostriches were trapped in the wild, raised on farms in vast flocks, and slaughtered in their hundreds of thousands.

As Australia possessed large tracts of habitat similar to the ostrich's native range of central and southern Africa and parts of Arabia, it was thought by those who imported them that they should do well here. It took some time to breed and raise sufficient numbers to enable the farmers to cash in on this lucrative market, for it takes three years for proper adult plumage to form, and even then, it is only the male's feathers that have high value. In any event it was thought well worth the effort. (A Queensland farmer is currently trying to re-establish this industry, from wild South Australian stock.)

It is unknown how successful the original breeding farms were since interest waned in this enterprise as the demand for feathers declined with the inevitable change in fashions. As a result, these birds were simply set free to fend for themselves in the wild.

Ostriches still occupy areas around Port Augusta in South Australia, which was the original site of many of the farms. Although the climate and habitat should have been to their liking, most failed to survive once released. It may have been that once set free, the native emu out-competed them for food and they became prey for dingoes.

Ostriches were never truly

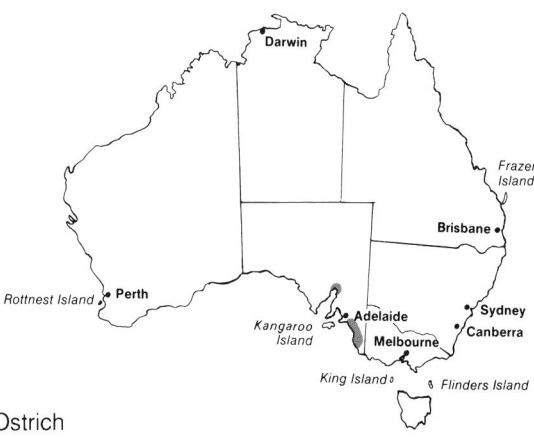

Ostrich

domesticated, and for that reason cannot now be classified as being 'feral'. They have always been, in Australia as in Africa, wild birds that have been fenced in.

Feral Turkey

Large flocks of turkeys currently run wild on Flinders Island in Bass Strait, off the Tasmanian coast. They originated from stock once held by soldier settlers who raised them for the table.

This island had many small farms which most often supported one family, however, in time the economics of farming caused small holdings to be amalgamated into larger properties. As this occurred

Feral Turkey

the turkeys, which were once closely husbanded, were allowed to wander at will. Certainly some of them were still taken for the table, although the majority were not so much set free but simply left to fend for themselves without supervision or control.

They number a few hundred on this large island, and it is quite startling to hear their gobbling call coming from thick ti-tree scrub which covers much of the uncleared areas there.

Feral Domestic Fowl

These birds bear only faint resemblance to our common domestic fowls of today as they have reverted to their wild form. There are only two known colonies in Australia.

On Northwest Island off the North Queensland coast these birds have run wild for almost a hundred years. The original birds were abandoned by Japanese labourers who had been phosphate mining on the island for a short period in the 1880s. The Japanese left in the 1890s, and it was not until 1924 that these birds were seen again, when a small group of people set up a turtle soup factory there which they ran for four years. The only people to visit the island since that time have been small numbers of holiday makers.

Recently, poultry researchers have trapped some of these birds so as to learn more about the natural forebears of our much hybridised modern fowl.

There is another flock that inhabits Goat Island in Sydney Harbour. It has been there since the early 1900s. Not much is known about them, except that they are a constant source of annoyance to residents of the nearby expensive waterfront homes, who regularly complain to the authorities about the noisy crowing of the roosters. There is the possibility of the existence of other colonies of feral domestic fowls in isolated areas, but they could only occur where they would not be subjected to predation by feral cats and foxes.

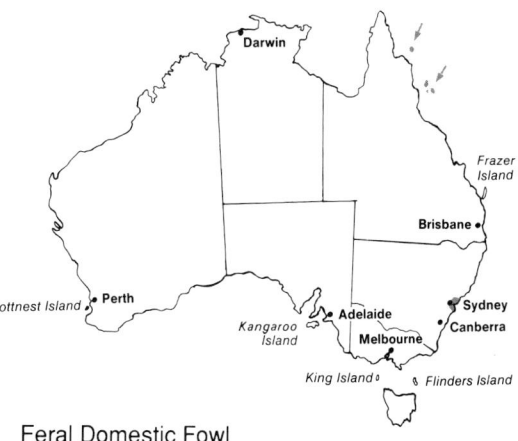

Feral Domestic Fowl

FISH

It would not have been long after their arrival that the new settlers would have begun to 'throw a line' into the waterways of this country just to see what could be had in the way of fish to eat, and perhaps to provide sport.

The majority of these early settlements were established in coastal areas; good catches of sea and estuary fish were obtained, although these were primarily for eating and not sporting purposes. The many rivers and streams that run from the Great Dividing Range (the early barrier to inland settlement) to the coast don't have a great variety of fish, and very few could be considered sporting in the English tradition.

English gentlemen have long been keen on the sport of angling. Many dress in tweed jackets and vests, and tuck their trousers into their stockings; they wear the appropriate hat, and most often a collar and tie. They have rods and lures that are made by craftsmen, and special lines to cast them with. To be so stylishly dressed and so particularly equipped, one surely requires a variety of fish deserving of such finery, and with a sporting nature, so as to be worthy of the effort.

In the 1860s, many settlers, having made great wealth from grazing, merchandising and other enterprises, took on the trappings of British gentry. They began to import the animals such gentlemen hunted, the pheasant, the fox and the deer. Fish were needed too, for one could not become a true gentleman and pursue angling without the appropriate fish. The brown trout of England and Europe was just such a fish. It was largely the exclusive fish of gentlemen; as ordinary folk were not thought worthy to fish for it. There were other fish for common folk, coarse fish: the dace, the roach and tench, amongst others.

All these fish thrived in the cold mountain-fed streams and rivers of the eastern coast of mainland Australia and in the waterways of Tasmania.

It was not until the 1860s, when the interior of this country was beginning to be discovered, that the explorers told of the fish they had encountered in the inland. Their journals recorded with praise the abundant cod, some of such size that it took two men to pull them to the bank, the fat yellowbelly that provided them with sumptuous feasts, and of a marvel of nature, when countless native spangled perch came wriggling and shimmering out of what had been parched earth and mud. Could it be, they pondered, that native fish live in the soil and only appear as water trickles over them?

The northern rivers were found to be home to the fish which put up the greatest fight, the barramundi, which also happened to be excellent to eat. These fighters are all born females, and remain so until four years of age; only with adulthood do sufficient numbers turn into males. This unusual life cycle is compounded by protection of the young in the parents mouths. They also learned of a fish in northern regions, the archer fish, so named because it uses water droplets to shoot down its prey from out of overhanging shrubs and bushes. There was even a fish in Queensland that breathed air, and so it was called the lungfish.

However, few, if any, of these fish met the requirement of being 'sporting fish'.

In any event, most of these native freshwater fish were found far from where the majority of the new immigrants chose to live. What they wanted were fish suitable for the cooler streams of the coastal settlements.

Introductions from Europe and other countries followed; the fighting rainbow trout and salmon from America, and of course, the Atlantic salmon, a fighting fish of great repute.

The importers went to great lengths and expense to bring these fish into Australia. They tried various methods to keep eggs alive on the three-month sea voyages. They experimented with running cold water over them to try and emulate the streams they came from. They tried gravel beds, moss-lined boxes, they even packed them in ice, yet again and again they lost their precious cargo and their money too. The problems that the acclimatisers faced were monumental, and if they had not been met with an equal measure of determination, these fish would not be here today.

Some twenty fish species have been introduced to this country; some were eagerly sought, whilst others were accidentally released. In any event, they now share our waterways with two hundred or so native species of freshwater and tidal reach fish. Of these new arrivals, some provide excellent sport, others are merely a nuisance, and some we could well do without.

Brown Trout

European brown trout were brought to this country in the 1860s and released into the cold mountain-fed streams of the east coast of south eastern mainland Australia and Tasmania. They were brought here to satisfy those who thought the streams of the first settlements here lacked fish of sporting interest and pleasant flavour.

The native freshwater fish that lived in these streams were strangers to the settlers from Europe; they did not know what bait or lures were needed to make them bite. Less was understood of their seasonal and breeding habits. On the other hand, they had long developed the sport in their homeland, for books had been in print as early as 1496 describing how best

to catch the trout.

Of all the European fish that settlers had been familiar with back home, it was the brown trout that they knew best. They had everything that anglers sought in a fish. They live in almost any cool water and readily breed there, so that they can be commonly found. They fight well on light tackle, and don't 'line up' to get on the hook, thus requiring the angler to use his wits in their capture. They range a good deal in size and so one can hope and anticipate that what is on the line is a big one. When the sporting contest is over, one is left with a fish that has a very acceptable eating quality.

The brown trout has captured the imagination of the world's anglers and has been introduced around the globe. It, more than any other fish, carries a certain mystique about it for all those who seek it. There is more written about it than other fish regarding its difficulty to catch, its feeding habits and its cunning and elusiveness. The brown trout is very much a slow water fish, for even in a fast flowing river it will choose to be out of the main current. It usually faces upstream and takes up a position in slack water, behind a submerged rock in the main stream, or lies close to the bank or in any other position where it has food washed to it. Thus it can take its time and be selective in its choice of food, and this habit has no doubt given rise to its reputation of being a finicky and selective feeder.

Fishing for trout in Britain has mostly been only for the wealthy or privileged as many stretches of water are under the control of one person. Fishing for the

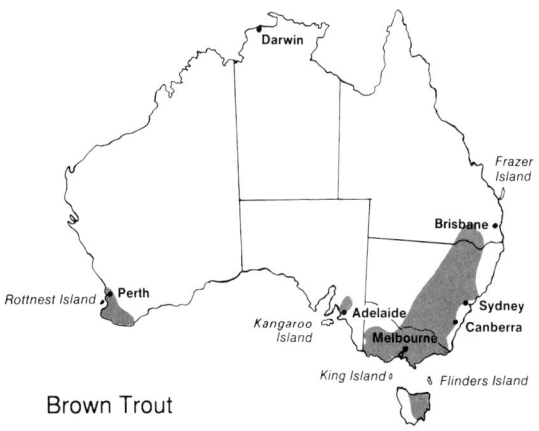

Brown Trout

brown trout in Australia can be enjoyed by all. It has grown into a big industry here and has attracted thousands of devotees. Here the trout are more numerous and their average size is larger than in Britain.

This fish has been introduced throughout southern and eastern Australia and to parts of Western Australia. It has been introduced to all waters that are suitable for it, to streams and rivers, natural lakes and particularly to water impoundments created for the development and generation of hydro-electric power (such as the Snowy Mountains Scheme in New South Wales). Brown trout are artificially raised in hatcheries and millions are released each year throughout Australia. Some fingerlings reach the waterways in tubs of water, transported by trucks, and they are simply tipped in, whilst others are flown to their destination and released from the plane as it flies above the water.

The purpose of stocking and re-stocking is to improve the harvest for anglers and the quantities of the species so introduced, whilst at the same time it is hoped to overcome the natural losses that occur due to predation and disease.

The long-term goal of stocking and re-stocking is to encourage the fish to breed at a sufficient rate to maintain numbers so that re-stocking will be needed only after severe drought, or when trout populations are decimated by other causes such as pollution, floods and overfishing.

Rainbow Trout

The rainbow trout is a native of North America, and has similar sporting and eating qualities to those of the brown trout. The rainbows differ in that they are fish of fast-flowing water, and consequently, to maintain a position in very fast flowing water they are forced to snap at anything they consider to be food as it rushes by. They are not selective or finicky feeders like European trout. Consequently they are considered by anglers to bite more freely and be easier to catch. However, they will not hesitate to spit anything out that they consider to be unpalatable.

They can grow to be very large fish, sixteen kilograms or more, although they average much less than this in Australia, where two to three kilograms would be a good-sized fish. However, the average in one Victorian lake is six kilograms.

In North America where they have the opportunity to 'run to sea', they prefer to do so, and they return later as a fish called a steelhead. When given this opportunity in Australia, they have failed to return.

Rainbow Trout

The rainbow trout is a very popular fish in Australia. It was released in many of the same areas as the brown trout. They spawn in rivers and their tributaries which run into land-locked lakes, but not all waters suit them, and for this reason they have not become as common or widespread as the brown trout.

Eastern Brook Trout

This fish is not a true trout but a member of the salmon family. It is a native of North America, and was released in Australia in the early 1900s.

Brook trout are more adaptable to widely varying conditions than other species and are able to spawn successfully in land-locked waters that do not have streams entering them.

The eastern brook trout are quick growers and are considered good biters. They are able to breed at a younger age than other trout species.

For these reasons it was hoped by authorities that the brook trout might

Eastern Brook Trout

thrive in waters unsuitable for other species and would not require continual re-stocking because of their adaptability and spawning habits. However, they only occur in a few waters in Tasmania and in limited areas of New South Wales, where they provide good sport on light tackle, although two kilograms and forty centimetres in length would be considered a very good fish.

Why they have not become more common and widespread is difficult to say. Perhaps it is their relatively small size and the fact that they cannot successfully compete with other trout species in shared waters; perhaps our waters lack some of their requirements.

Atlantic Salmon

The Atlantic salmon was a more exclusive fish of the sporting aristocracy of Britain than the brown trout, for the waters that contained these large (fourteen kilograms/one hundred and twenty centimetres), silvery, tenacious fighters were strictly controlled and were only available to the privileged few who could afford to pay the rights to fish for them.

From the early 1900s, both private individuals and fishing authorities tried to establish this fish in Australia. They had success growing the salmon here, although when they were released into streams that would allow them to 'run to sea', they always failed to return.

The Atlantic salmon have evolved to migrate from the streams of their natural range of North America, Scandinavia and the United Kingdom, travelling distances of some five hundred kilometres to live and feed on krill, a small shrimp-like creature in the oceans of the northern hemisphere. It is still not fully known how they manage their incredible navigation.

Atlantic Salmon

Are they guided by the currents or the stars? It is known that they are able to retain a smell and taste of the water of their native streams, for although they may live for years in the sea, they are able to unerringly return to the very stream in which they were born.

It was surely too much to expect from the Atlantic salmon that they would set off from Australia to locate their traditional feeding grounds halfway across the globe, and then return. So it certainly would have been surprising if this fish became permanently established in Australia.

They have an important advantage over other salmon species in that they do not die after spawning. Efforts are still being made to permanently establish the Atlantic salmon in landlocked waters in Australia.

Quinnat Salmon

The quinnat salmon is a North American fish that was first introduced to Australia in the 1960s and, like the Atlantic salmon, it failed to return from the sea when released.

The quinnat is also known as the chinook, king or pacific salmon. They are native to the Columbia River of Oregon.

Quinnat Salmon

Quinnat salmon were re-introduced to Australia in 1966 to Lake Purrumbete, a land-locked body of water in western Victoria. Whilst these salmon will not actually breed or bear young in land-locked water, the females will ripen and so produce ova, and likewise the male will produce milt. This ripening allows for them to be netted and milked of their contents, so that hatcheries are able to artificially breed new stocks.

This small lake of fifty-five hectares is seasonally opened to fishing whereupon an instant 'tent city' springs up as some four thousand anglers and a thousand boats crowd the water to catch these two to three kilogram silvery salmon.

In America and New Zealand, where they run to sea, Quinnat salmon are fighting fish of great repute, and of a good size; commonly four kilograms to twenty kilograms, (some of forty-five kilograms). It is unfortunate that they are unable to provide us here with the same degree of sporting fight.

New Zealand has been able to successfully establish the quinnat salmon in wild rivers of the South Island that empty their contents of melted snow into the ocean, and now have a forty million dollar export industry.

European Perch or Redfin

The European perch is a freshwater fish which has an attractive, colourful appearance. It has become better known in Australia as the redfin, because of the characteristic colour of its fins.

This fish can show great variation in body colouring from dark grey to blue, yellowish or the more common olive on the back. Their bellies are usually whitish in colour and there are usually up to seven distinct stripes or bars on their sides, varying in colour from black to red or golden yellow.

They do not have a streamlined shape, being relatively broad and deep with a high back; this body shape suits their natural habitat, the large, slow-moving rivers of Europe.

The redfin was introduced as a sporting fish, although perhaps it would be more correctly described as a fish that may offer some sport. It was not classified as a game fish by the anglers from Europe, as they didn't consider this perch to be worthy of their time. Redfin are a predatory fish and will bite freely and boldly. They very often school which allows for good catches, for as soon as one is hooked, repeated casts in the same spot will often bring forth many more.

Large numbers of anglers in Australia fish for the redfin exclusively, preferring the brisk action fishing and the almost guaranteed meal this fish provides when compared to the finicky and temperamental trout. Many who catch them class their flesh as being superior to any other.

The redfin is a very capable breeder, and one that is capable of easily maintaining itself without much assistance from the authorities—too easily, some say, for their eradication in some waters has proved not only expensive, but all but impossible. They breed at the relatively young age of twelve months and can produce an enormous number of eggs for their size, sometimes almost as many as two hundred thousand in a two kilogram fish. As well, their eggs have a high survival rate compared to other freshwater fish. Rather than their ova being at the mercy of the elements, they are protected and contained in a metre long, ribbon-like, sticky transparent mass that readily adheres to water plants and, snags for the relatively short time of seven to twenty days until they are hatched.

The redfin is found throughout the cooler slow waters of rivers, lakes, farm dams and other man-made water storages in Victoria, New South Wales, South Australia and Western Australia. Their

occupation of such waters results from both deliberate and accidental releases.

In some states the authorities suggest that the redfin became accidentally introduced to many waters when their sticky egg mass attached to the feet and bodies of migrating waterfowl. It is also known that commercial hatcheries have, on occasions, inadvertently allowed the fertilised ova of redfin to contaminate orders of other fish, their ova and young. Anglers, too, have shifted the redfin from one water to another to provide fishing somewhere new, and to use them as 'bait' in catching other species.

Coarse Fish: Tench, Roach and Dace

'Coarse fishing' is the term given to angling for these species of fish and for other members of the carp family. Whether this is a description of the nature of the fish, having firm flesh covered in large hard scales, or a term given by the ruling classes of Europe to define a sport less refined than trout fishing, or even descriptive of the manners and attitudes of those who fished for them, is unknown.

However, the tench and other coarse species were historically the common people's fish, and popular ones, in Britain and throughout Europe. All of these fish provided a free and tasty meal and some,

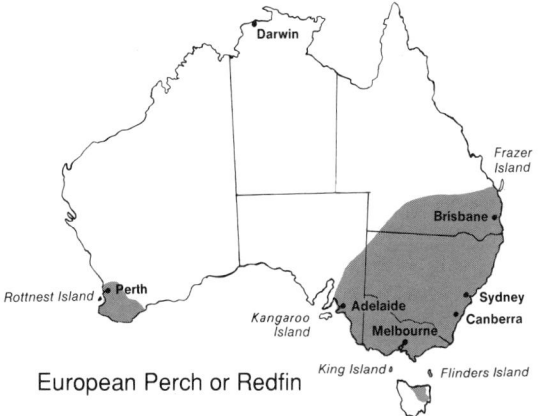

European Perch or Redfin

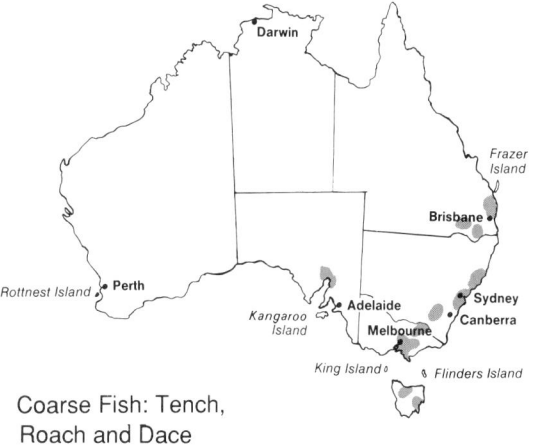

Coarse Fish: Tench, Roach and Dace

it was said, possessed healing powers over those forced to angle for them.

Their release in Australia, which began most probably only shortly after the first settlements and before introductions of sporting fish, was to fill the role they had in the immigrants' home countries. Nowadays, few people would fish for them as they offer little in the way of sport, and they have found little favour as a table fish.

Nevertheless the tench and roach have become relatively widespread, particularly in the lower Murray and Darling river systems, and in many waterways in Tasmania.

Tench

The tench is a sluggish fish preferring still water, such as in dams and ponds, slow moving rivers, or the quieter deep holes of those that run fast. The muddy water of swamps don't deter it for, like other carp, the tench is equipped with barbels, or feelers, which allow it to find its way, and to feed by sifting the mud for small creatures and plant life.

Tench can grow to be large fish, some as big as seventy centimetres in length, and four and a half kilograms in weight, although half a kilogram is the norm. The tench is most easily recognised by the circle of red around their protruding eyes and mouth.

Although tench lack the large hard scales of other coarse species, they nevertheless qualify for this group by the slimy nature of their bodies, which are dark olive green on the back and sides, running into shades of gold and pink on the belly.

Roach

The roach is yet another carp, and it was released in much the same localities as the tench and for the same reasons.

The roach is more like the tench than the common carp, in that it has a very small mouth and humped back, with the red outer colouring around the eyes.

It is usually a dark grey colour on the back and head, with blue-green shading of the sides running to a somewhat paler colouring of silver on the belly. The fin colour of the roach can vary from a brassy yellow, or rust and orange colour, to red.

Roach are also a slow water fish. They feed in the same manner as other carp, and have a similar diet.

Dace

Dace are small fish, few exceeding thirty centimetres in length. They have a metallic sheen to their blue-black back. Their sides and belly are whitish yellow. Their uppermost fins are a uniform grey, whereas those of the lower body are of orange-red to pale yellow. They are also identified by their distinctive forked tail.

Dace have similar food preferences to those of the trout, namely insects both in the water and above, and waterborne aquatic creatures including worms, snails and insect larvae.

Dace were certainly introduced and released in waters about Sydney, Melbourne and in various areas of Tasmania. However, little is reported of them nowadays, most probably because few people can identify them accurately as they are easily confused with the many carp species that have become all too common in our waterways.

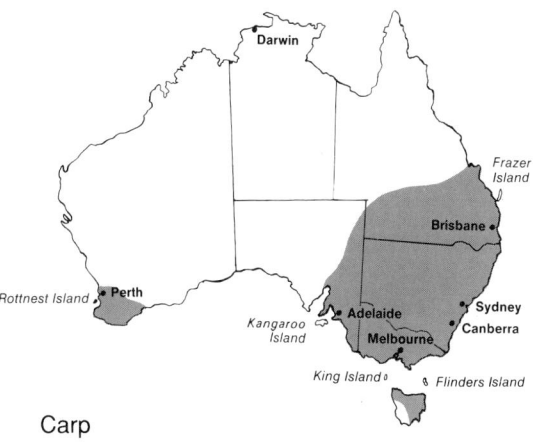

Carp

Carp

At least five species of carp have been introduced to Australia and these were released into freshwater rivers, dams, lakes and other waterways both intentionally and accidentally. At least one or more carp species have become relatively widespread in every state of Australia.

Carp are natives of central Asia and China, although they were spread throughout Europe from the very early times. They were most often kept and bred in captivity as a farmed or cultivated food source. They were particularly important during the long periods of Lent when eating meat was proscribed by religious beliefs. To a lesser extent they were used as ornamental creatures.

Most species of carp prefer relatively warm water that is shallow and muddy on the bottom. Waters such as these usually provide abundant plant growth which harbours a rich variety of water insects and their larvae, including fresh-water shrimps, worms and snails. As most carp have barbels or feelers which protrude from the area of the mouth, they are able to use these as organs of touch and to assist in grubbing and sifting through the mud. Carp have teeth in their throat rather than in the mouth. They take in mud and other particles, retaining and swallowing the food whilst at the same time getting rid of the mud and other matter that is not required.

Waterways such as those described provide ideal breeding conditions for carp, as warm shallow waters with abundant weed growth may encourage them to breed up to six times per year. They are able to breed at a rate far in excess of most other fish; they lay more eggs than trout or salmon, usually a hundred times more, and they lay their long sticky ribbons of them in much safer situations where they are less affected by changes in water temperature, pollution and flooding.

It is little realised by anglers in Australia today, who predominantly fish for trout and consider the carp a pest, in what regard the carp was held by many of our first settlers. Many were from the working classes of Europe, who had not enjoyed privileges reserved for the gentry which included fishing for trout and salmon. It is certain that the majority of early immigrants would have been familiar with catching and eating carp, and this familiarity would have played a major role in their initial release and widespread distribution.

Carp have also been spread by migratory waterbirds, and by being mixed in with other fish and fertilised ova as they were trapped and introduced into new waters. Many other releases have

been deliberate, such as those in irrigation country, where the carp are used to keep the channels clear of water weeds. Fishermen have long used them to catch the Murray cod; they are an ideal bait for they travel very well, only requiring to be kept moist to live. They last a long time on a hook and are a lively, active bait to tempt the cod. Unused bait was very often simply tipped into the river, either to save taking it home and having to dispose of it, or to provide a handy source of bait fish on future trips. Carp are easily caught for bait and, who knows, the cod may grow bigger by eating them.

Even though the authorities spent vast

sums of money trying to eradicate the carp, and although they impose heavy fines on those caught with live fish in their possession, they have not halted the travel of this hardy and adaptable fish.

Many carp find their way to the city markets where they are eagerly sought by people who ate them in their homelands. Many people make a living by selling them to commercial piggeries or canneries. Some electrocute vast quantities of them in rivers, from a power source in their rowboats, others are netted.

There is a great variety of carp, and what is termed the common carp is difficult to define. Some are thirty centimetres long, whilst others can be a metre in length and twenty-five kilograms in weight; nearly all have barbels on the lip, and large, hard scales. Their colour varies greatly, although they are usually a dark olive-green on the back with paler bluish glints on the sides and the belly is yellow or brassy gold. The fins are usually blue-green, often toned with red. The crucian carp, a well known species, is very similar in colour to other carp, although they almost always have a dark spot at the base of the tail.

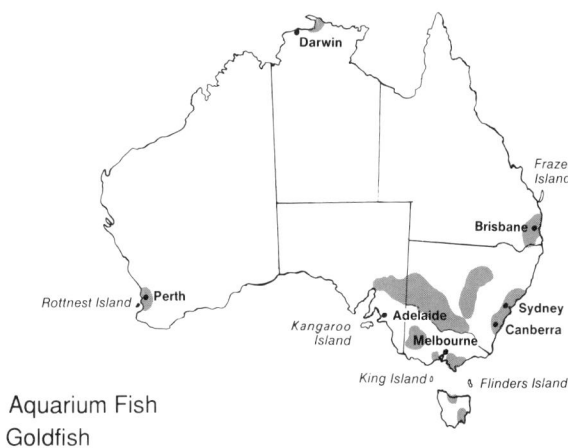

Aquarium Fish
Goldfish

Probably the main reason that goldfish have become so numerous and widespread here is that eggs or the young were accidentally introduced as a result of being mixed with other carp that were released deliberately. Unintentional releases may have occurred as a result of goldfish being used as bait fish to catch other species, and some have gained their freedom when they were simply tipped from their aquariums into the waterways.

Goldfish

Goldfish are another variety of carp which have become numerous and widespread, particularly in certain areas of southern Australia. However, in the wild they differ greatly in appearance from the ornamental breed that is commonly kept as aquarium pets.

The common domestic variety has been selectively bred over centuries to become a popular ornamental fish worldwide, with its long fluttering tail and small overall size. The goldfish that live in the wild here, in rivers and dams, more closely resemble the Asian wild carp from which the domestic aquarium fish originated.

Goldfish in the wild readily interbreed with other carp and lose their identifying features, becoming what are termed common carp. They have large, coarse scales, humped backs and small mouths. Because of their interbreeding they can be almost any size and can show great variation in colour but are most commonly brassy gold or red.

Aquarium Fish

Many other species of small aquarium fish now occur in areas of most states in Australia. They were released mainly because they were no longer required for aquariums.

Most are popular ornamental breeds, such as the guppy, the paradise fish, the swordtail and the leopard fish, natives of Asia and Africa.

Fortunately, to date the diseases aquarium fish sometimes carry have not infected our native fish, but the threat is ever present.

It is understandable that some people are loath to kill their pets when circumstances arise which make them unable to care for them any longer. However, great damage is done to the waterways of Australia, and to the creatures that live in them, by such careless and inappropriate disposal of unwanted aquarium fish and plants.

Mosquito Fish or Gambusia

This very small fish, only about fifty millimetres long, is a native of the Middle East, Asia and the Americas. It was brought to Australia in the 1930s, and released in perhaps more waterways than any other fish that has been introduced to this country.

Both the army and local councils were vigorous in their efforts to establish this fish in most states, as it was considered that it might control mosquitoes on which it feeds. Mosquitoes were becoming of increasing concern; serious diseases such as malaria were being spread by them, and were increasing to epidemic proportions at the time.

Malaria was relatively unknown in Australia and had little impact on the general population here, until servicemen who had been fighting overseas returned home infected with this disease.

These little fish were spread throughout our northern regions, the eastern states and probably in other states as well. The gambusia breed prolifically, often having up to sixty young at a time, and they are able to breed several times a year in ideal conditions. More importantly, rather than have their eggs subject to the ravages of

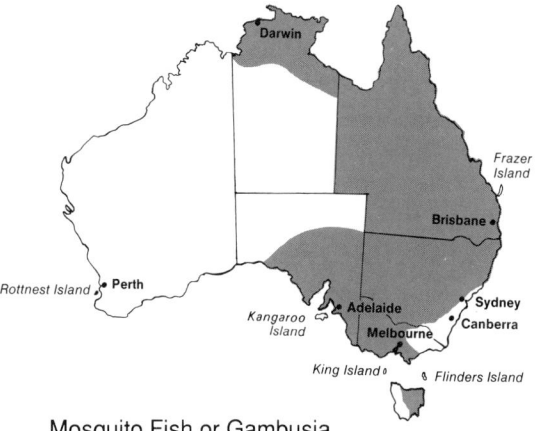

Mosquito Fish or Gambusia

nature and predators, the female bears live young from a pouch at the rear of her body, and allows them to retreat to her mouth whenever danger threatens.

Pacific Oyster

The Pacific oyster was introduced to Port Sorrell on Tasmania's north-west coast by a government research organisation in 1948 in order to test their adaptability to Tasmania's cold waters. If successful, it was expected that they would provide the basis for an oyster farming industry.

Whilst the native Sydney rock oyster is a valuable and sought after shellfish, its particular requirements of habitat make for limited growing areas, scarcity and consequently high prices. The constantly increasing demand for oysters certainly encouraged the Tasmanian experiment.

Pacific Oyster

From their initial release point, this oyster has drifted with tides and colonised many large areas, some being forty-eight kilometres from their original source. The razor sharpness of their shells has proved a hazard, particularly along shorelines that were popular for bathing and boating. In some localities they have become a serious pest. The colonising habits of this shellfish have caused the authorities to grant licences to individuals to farm or culture them on the condition that the licencees be responsible for any spread and consequent clean up required.

Whether this condition placed on the farming of the Pacific oyster is responsible for the fluctuating nature of the industry is difficult to gauge.

INSECTS

Insects, because of their small size, most often hardly receive a second glance, yet there are more species of insects throughout the world than all the groups of animals put together.

Australia is a very old continent, and in its isolation it has evolved a seemingly endless wealth of insects and other unique small creatures. There are some sixteen hundred species of flies, many thousands of beetles, a whole host of bugs and a myriad of other small creatures. We possess so many varieties, in fact, that to date, some fifty-four thousand species have been recorded, twice as many as we knew of only forty years ago, and in all probability there are still many more yet to be discovered.

Australia certainly had sufficient native insects and small creatures and had no need to share the countryside with the countless others that were introduced. Yet, from the first landings of ships in Australia, many more were added, as foreign creatures came aboard ships bound for our shores from ports around the globe in a multitude of ways, both as adults and as eggs. Some would have come in amongst the badly needed plants and vegetables, and in the soil which surrounded their roots. There were bugs in bedding, weevils in grain, cockroaches in pantries, fleas and lice and clothes moths amongst clothes. Silverfish hid in papers and books; possibly they were in the folds of the very charts which showed the way to Australia. There was a host of other small creatures and insects that were carried by people, their belongings, and in every nook and cranny of the ships, including their cargo and provisions.

Most of these insects and other small creatures simply gained entry to Australia down the gangplanks of ships, along with the convicts, immigrants and new settlers, their livestock, plants and baggage.

Had our new settlers realised the consequences of such introductions, they might have taken the opportunity afforded by the long sea voyages to track down and get rid of many troublesome creatures. This land could have been a virtual paradise without them. But alas, little thought was given to such matters then.

So it was, that with every plant brought into this country, the troublesome unwanted insects and other small creatures that lived amongst them came in too.

Insect pests were introduced with plants, so that aphids attacked the rose blooms in Australia as they had done for centuries in England. Likewise, the little pink and white caterpillar of the infamous codling moth drills unerringly into the core of the apple, and then exits by

The Codling Moth.

consuming the tasty white flesh, so spoiling the fruit in our country as it does throughout Europe.

The humble potato has its moth, similarly the cabbage. Other creatures which have found their way to our shores,

The Cabbage Moth.

like the mole cricket with its powerful front legs, and the earwig, much feared for its rear pincers and preference for human ears, appear not at all fussy about what they eat in our gardens and orchards.

The silvery trails about our gardens left by the common European garden snail are all too common. These creatures seem hell bent on nibbling our most prized garden plants and crops. Although these widespread 'land snails', as they are most correctly termed, are the most common, Australia is now the home of many of their cousins, notably the garden slug, the yellow and white snail and a more recent invader, the giant African snail. This colossus amongst snails can be over half a kilogram in weight, and some twenty-five centimetres long. It has, it is hoped, been recaptured after its brief escape.

As so much of the vegetation planted in the areas in which we live is introduced, we have provided the ideal surroundings for old world insects and small creatures. They prosper, become prolific and widespread. So thorough has the introduction of plants and the creatures hidden amongst them been that any insect specimen commonly seen is more likely to be a foreigner than a native. It might be the small, grey and armadillo-like slater or wood louse. Or the red, black and orange harlequin bug, which has the peculiar habit of taking it in turns with another to grasp the hind legs and then tow each other around on leaves.

The creepy crawlies around our houses are almost always creatures of other lands. Few of us realise this when we claim the flies are bad, or complain of damaging holes left by the clothes moth. When we confront the mess left amongst books and papers by the powdery silverfish, we see them as creatures that are part and parcel of everyday life and assume that they have always been a nuisance in Australia.

There is a tiny ant from the Argentine that is so small it can hardly be seen, but it has proved capable of invading and damaging our houses and buildings. The Indian termite has caused such damage that to eradicate them whole buildings in the national capital of Canberra have had to be encased in plastic sheets and fumigated. After dark, torchlight will reveal stealthy cockroaches which came from America, Europe and Asia.

These creatures, along with many other imports of their kind, lurk amongst the cracks and crevices of our buildings where they raid and spoil our foodstuffs and spread diseases. Although we have waged a continual war against them (and allowed the pest control companies to become multimillion dollar industries), we don't seem to be gaining ground in control of them. Still we arm ourselves with sprays, poison baits, hideous chemicals, traps, lures and the ever-present napthalene which we spread about our stored clothing and materials.

Over many centuries such creatures have become so adept at living with people that they can almost be described as domesticated. As Europeans travelled the world and set up house, so did these creatures that we share our Australian homes with. Had these same creatures arrived of their own accord, before European settlement, the Aborigines' nomadic lifestyle would have offered no shelter to them. The Aborigines had no larder, so necessary for the cockroach. Introduced creatures could not have stood the hardships of this way of life but they have learned to take advantage of our

European lifestyle.

Domestic animals including cattle, sheep, pigs, goats and horses, working dogs and pet dogs, cats, and every type of poultry were introduced within a short time of the founding of the colony. Whilst they were all welcome, apparently no thought was given to them as hosts of insects and the other small creatures they carried on and in themselves.

Horses stepped ashore with bots (the wriggling larvae of a large striped fly) in their nostrils and stomachs, or they had the eggs of them securely fastened to the hairs of their legs or bodies. No sooner had the stables been erected than the European stable fly made its unwelcome appearance. The large grey water buffalo brought in its own blood-sucking fly, which quickly learned to enjoy the blood of European cattle. Poultry, craved by the settlers for both their eggs and tasty flesh, brought ticks in amongst their feathers. The dogs and cats had a tick of their own, and there was a special flea for each of them too, as well as mites of various kinds. All these exotics affected them in this new land as they had done in their countries of origin.

Cattle and other livestock were similarly affected, not only by the great numbers of creatures that were on their bodies, but hidden in their interiors as well. Many of these have evolved over centuries to live as parasites, a normal and usual relationship.

We know little of what we cannot see and whilst the study of parasites may seem an unpleasant one to some people, it is nevertheless an important and interesting part of nature.

There is a tapeworm which lives in the intestines of domestic cats and dogs as well as foxes, which can infect people. The mature parasite lays eggs in its host which pass out with the droppings; when they come into contact with water, they hatch and the larvae are eaten by a particular water flea. The microscopic larvae, once inside the flea's stomach, burrow through into the body cavity, where they undergo a second larvae stage. The life cycle, in order to continue, requires that the water flea be eaten either by a lizard, snake, frog, tadpole, rabbit, mouse, rat or pig (all intermediate hosts). For the third stage of the larvae to develop, they must burrow through the intestines of the host, and locate themselves in tissues between the creature's muscles. It is like a worm now, about ten centimetres long, and there can be many of them. In order for these to develop into the final stage of the adult tapeworm, and thus complete the cycle, the infested intermediate host, must be eaten by a final host, the domestic dog, cat or fox.

Should the tapeworm not go through all of these precise stages, each of them in turn, nothing will become of it, and one would think that such a complicated procedure provided ample opportunity for a break to occur in this complex chain. Yet, this parasite is still with us and presumably it will continue to be.

Man becomes involved by eating inadequately cooked meat of the feral pig. Pig shooters sometimes eat their kill, and there are those who trap wild pigs and fatten them up for others to eat. There is an increasing possibility that this disease called sparganosis, will become more common and widespread in humans should domestic pigs be allowed to forage in swampy areas where frogs and water fleas abound, and which may be visited by the fox or domestic cat or dog.

Livestock transported to this country mixed with animals from other lands with which they had no previous contact. There was consequently a mixing of insects too, many of which chose to live on creatures that they had never known before. Many so enjoyed their new hosts that they have remained with them up until the present day.

Whilst the settlers preferred familiar cattle such as Hereford, Angus, Guernsey, a small number of Zebu cattle were brought from Java to Darwin in the mid 1800s, not for breeding, but for slaughter. The cattle ticks which came in with them quickly attached themselves to the bodies of the European breeds. Asian cattle harbour these ticks but they are immune to the fever they cause, whereas European breeds had no such resistance and they began to lose condition and very often died.

It was this new association which created the problem. Parasites which evolve with their hosts over a long period of time usually strike a balance of living at the hosts' expense, although most often they do not damage them to a serious or life-threatening degree. This ensures the survival and continuance of each species, so that each may prosper.

The cattle tick caused such serious losses amongst European breeds in northern Australia that it reduced cattle numbers by half. Many methods were tried to rid cattle of these blood-sucking creatures. Whole areas had become tick infested, which required enforced control of stock movements. Fences were built and constantly patrolled to stop cattle from straying to clean or uninfested areas. Cattle were dipped, sprayed, jetted and inoculated, and even a particular bird (the cattle egret) was introduced, as it was known to eat this pest. Yet still the tick survived to continue its damaging work, and it is claimed to be the most costly parasite ever to affect Australian primary production.

It is indeed ironic that when all control measures had met with only limited success, further importations of the very species of cattle which brought this tick in were made necessary. The zebu, brahman and other humped species of Asian cattle were introduced in ever increasing numbers, either to displace or cross with European breeds.

The explorers and others who discovered land beyond the settlements, were so enthusiastic about the new-found abundant and bountiful grazing lands, ideally suited to sheep, that they sent letters by the score back to England so that breeding stock could be quickly dispatched. Sheep were eagerly sent, and Britain encouraged this trade; it already had in place vast manufacturing mills that could make good use of cheap wool. Good profit could also be made by those who brought sheep of different breeds from all regions of the old world, trusting that some may ideally suit the climate and conditions of this new land. Some breeds were selected for their wool, others more for their meat.

Every comfort was afforded the sheep during transport on board the ships for they were valuable stock. Yet not much thought was given to the fact that most were carrying the very diseases and parasites that were of serious concern to their health in the regions from which they came. Like the horse, sheep had bots in their nostrils, keds and lice in their fleeces, as well as a great variety of internal parasites. Whilst some of these infestations are difficult to see, their symptoms were well known to the shepherds who had tended sheep similarly affected in Europe. The shepherds can perhaps be excused for not taking steps to eliminate such afflictions before the sheep were landed, for they had long become used to sheep having such diseases and parasites that they most probably considered them abnormal without them. So once flocks started building up in number, both the graziers and the shepherds would have expected some losses amongst their sheep. However, they were quite unprepared for the alarming number of sheep injured or killed due to fly-strike.

Flies were something immigrants very quickly became aware of, for the big hairy brown and yellow native blowflies soon made their presence felt by buzzing and bombarding any foodstuffs left uncovered. The little native bushflies also became apparent by their habit of alighting and clinging in their hundreds to the bodies of those who ventured outdoors.

However it was not the native blowflies or the sticky little bushflies that caused the problem of fly-strike in sheep. The blame rests with yet another accidental introduction, the European sheep greenbottle fly.

This troublesome fly probably avoided detection in our country for a long time as they are easily confused with a number of native flies which possess the same metallic green colouring. The great difference between these introduced greenbottles and the native blowflies is in their method of operation. The native blowflies had evolved with kangaroos, wombats and other animals that mostly possess hair-covered leathery skins, and these flies seemed never to learn how to penetrate this barrier. They had to rely on some injury being caused before they could gain entry to the flesh whilst the animal was alive. Because of this, the main function of the native blowflies was to be part of nature's 'clean-up brigade', mostly by living on dead animals (carrion). The greenbottles, however, having evolved amongst sheep, were equipped with the means to penetrate their soft skins, and so initiate a wound or strike themselves. This difference is an important one, because the greenbottle can cause wounds, and in so doing they create the ideal opportunity for the native blowflies to do their damaging work. The result is a far more extensive and serious wound than was first made by the greenbottle.

So, with the coming of sheep and greenbottle flies to this country, our native flies have been able to take advantage of a new food source and breeding medium. This has caused a great increase in their numbers and consequently a serious economic effect on the sheep industry. It appears that the introduced greenbottle and the native blowflies have formed a working relationship, one species depending on the other, and it is further claimed that the natives have learned how to penetrate the sheep's soft skin on their own. However, generally they still only provide a second wave attack.

Nevertheless, flies have created the need for many expensive control measures to limit the costly effects of fly strike.

Some insects have been deliberately introduced and one of the most important of these has been the European honey bee.

Australia was originally found to contain a number of species of native bees. They were generally small and had evolved alongside other creatures like sugar possums, honey-eating birds and a host of other insects to serve the peculiar and particular characteristics of Australian nectar-bearing native plants. Most people consider the only role of the bee is to produce honey whereas nature's role for the bee is to aid in the fertilisation of plants.

It is an important role that the bee performs, for when scientists put them to

The Silkworm, larvae of the Emperor Moth.

the test, they found that when bees were prevented from reaching the flowers in a small grove of pear trees it yielded only seven pears, and yet when they were allowed access to a similar number of adjoining trees, they bore four hundred fruits, a true measure of the worth of this tireless little worker.

Since its introduction the honey bee has done Australia great service pollinating our garden plants and a great range of flowers. By the setting of the fruit in our orchards and crops, the bee has allowed us to grow amounts large enough to both feed ourselves and to export the surplus to the countries from which the bee and our forefathers came. Of course it also produces honey which is claimed to be the oldest and purest of foods, and we also export a great deal of that.

The bee, although considered domesticated or controlled, is allowed to fly where it likes. Because of this freedom there is a continual escape of bees. Sometimes whole colonies may leave a congested hive to establish themselves in the wild in tree hollows, caves and elsewhere.

The honey bee was not the only insect or small creature that was deliberately introduced at the time of settlement. The Japanese silkworm was another. It was brought to Australia from Japan in the hope of establishing a silk industry which would provide valuable clothing material and employ many people as well.

I wonder if those who proposed the silkworm's introduction were aware of the Australian silkworm. We have a native, the Emperor gum moth, whose colourful caterpillar spins a cocoon of silk similar to that of the Asian silkworm. There are brown hairy caterpillars of the Inland that construct their thirty centimetre long communal cocoons in the mulga trees. They seem to be silken, but they too, may never have been tried as a commercial producer.

In any event, the foreign silkworms adapted and established themselves remarkably well in many areas of this country, as they had done previously in Japan, France and Turkey, and this was largely due to the importing and planting of their favoured food trees. Both the white fruited mulberry tree and the ailanthus tree were widely planted; the latter especially as a shade tree in hot areas, where it has since been declared noxious due to its free seeding nature. Both trees flourished and were quickly seen to attract the small creamy brown silkworm moths.

It is at this pupa or cocoon stage of its development that the people of the orient learned to intervene in the life cycle of the silkworm. They take the cocoons and place them in hot ovens so as to kill the pupae. Next comes the time-consuming task of unravelling the thousand metres of continuous silken thread of each cocoon. The total process of the production of silk, or sericulture as it is termed, is a long and involved one. It may have been the important stage of unwinding the cocoon, a delicate and time-consuming task, which caused the demise of this industry in Australia.

Although the silkworms prospered, as did the trees on which they fed, the industry never really took off.

Another insect brought into this country expressly in the hope of making a profit from its culture was the cochineal scale insect. The British had long been using the crimson dye cochineal, obtained from the crushed bodies of these insects, to colour their soldier's red coats. However, they were forced to obtain supplies of it from Portugal and Spain who had a monopoly of its culture and production. These two countries were very protective of this lucrative industry, so much so that they cleverly supplied their own soldiers with uniforms of other colours, thereby ensuring that most cochineal produced was available for export sales. They also restricted others from obtaining the particular type of prickly pear that this insect seemed to thrive on, much to the annoyance of England.

The eminent botanist Sir Joseph Banks, was thought to have proposed that the cochineal industry was ideally suited to Australian conditions and as the raw materials were unobtainable from the Spanish or Portuguese, it was suggested that Captain Phillip's First Fleet call into Brazil on its way to Australia and obtain specimens there. However, the cochineal insect failed to do well here on the Brazilian cacti, so further varieties were obtained in India and elsewhere. This was still to no avail, for whilst the cacti did well, the insect did not, and without its survival there could be no industry.

The prickly pear was later found to have other uses, such as in hedges for stock control and as a plant with edible fruits. The very insect which fed on the prickly pear failed to thrive, so that the plant flourished and spread in a rapid and alarming manner.

A special government board was set up for its eradication. In time after other methods of eradication had failed, the decision was made to investigate the new field of biological control, introducing natural enemies to pests. The board made detailed enquiries throughout the world for creatures which might prove effective against the prickly pear. Many insects were tried and the cochineal insect was reintroduced; but again, it only achieved limited success. However the creature which showed the greatest promise was the cactoblastis moth from the Argentine. It lays its eggs on the prickly pear and, on hatching, the banded grubs or larvae live on the juices of the plant, which they obtain by burrowing in its tissues; the tunnels they create as a result cause the plant's structure to collapse.

After successful trials in 1926, the cactoblastis was cultivated in sheds that were specially built on the site of heavy pear infestations. Millions of eggs were obtained, and by causing the moths to lay their eggs on small sections of paper, these could then be mailed to all areas of infestations. The egg-laden paper strips were simply speared on the pear plant by using a broken off spine from the cactus; it was a simple but effective means of distribution.

As soon as the cactoblastis became abundant and widespread in the field, its effect on the prickly pear was seen to be astounding in its completeness, for the massive plants seemed to simply crumple in its wake. It took only six years for the prickly pear to be nothing more than a rapidly decaying pulp upon the ground. Over twenty million hectares of land could be grazed and farmed once more.

Feelings ran so strongly in appreciation of the humble moth, that in one place a church service was held in its honour and the church was renamed the Cactoblastis Hall.

Even today the cactoblastis continues to serve; no sooner does a pear plant appear than it is cut down from within by the little banded grub.

The use of the cactoblastis as a biological control agent was a fantastic success, and completely justified this new and particular means of pest control in Australia. It demonstrated it had the four requirements of a control agent: it was effective; it proved to be cheaper in the long run than other means; it was host specific or did not harm anything else; and most importantly, it would not become a pest itself.

The advantages and effectiveness of biological control was clearly evident, yet authorities were still sceptical, and remained unconvinced for almost thirty years after the cactoblastis experiment that such a means of control would work against the rabbit.

It was the 1950s before the myxomatosis virus was tried as a biological means to control the rabbit. Even then, most remained unenthusiastic as to its likely effectiveness until, virtually overnight, it began to devastate the rabbit population; in just three years after its release, the rabbit was almost completely wiped out in Australia.

However, whilst the myxomatosis virus was effective, having a potential kill rate of ninety-nine per cent, its spreading agent, the mosquito, was proving unreliable in its role. Conditions had to be ideal for them, and they did not live in all areas that the rabbit did. So although the mosquitoes would carry the infecting virus to the rabbits that lived about their range in the summer months, the rabbits would quickly replace their own numbers during their winter breeding period. In areas where there were no mosquitoes, such as the hot dry plains of the inland and the snowline of our highest mountains, the rabbits did as they liked.

The mosquitoes just could not cope with the rabbits' extensive range, nor affect their breeding rate out of the summer months. As the effectiveness of the mosquito as a carrying agent of this virus began to wane, it became obvious that if rabbits were to be reduced and brought under control once and for all, a new different carrier needed to be found, one that was capable of being effective year round, in all climates and conditions, and most importantly, in all areas in which there were rabbits.

This led to the introduction of the European rabbit flea in 1966, which lives on the rabbit and goes wherever it goes. Scientists had discovered that this tiny flea's habit of breeding and living off the blood of pregnant female rabbits ensured a much more reliable and effective means of transmitting this disease.

This virus causes what can only be described as a horrible disease. It is cruel to cause this suffering, but necessary as it is the only recent method of control that has had any dramatic effect on the rabbit population. No country in the world has ever experienced the degree of damage that this one animal caused in Australia. There was damage to people and their livelihood, but it caused suffering to so many other creatures as well by destroying their habitat or food source, and in most cases, both. These creatures became victims of the multitude of control measures that were aimed at the rabbit.

The rabbit flea has in time proved so effective that there is a continuous ongoing programme of their culture. Once the fleas are artificially bred and infected with the virus, they are frozen and packaged in plastic containers ready for dispatch to areas of rabbit infestations.

Over the years rabbits have built up some immunity or resistance to the original form of myxomatosis but the scientists are able to engineer or manipulate this virus into various strains, which will probably continue to prove effective.

The various breeds of cattle, all being introduced animals, have since their arrival been a major source of Australia's wealth from the export of their dairy produce, meat and hides. Australia now has some twenty million head of cattle. Their sheer numbers have had a dramatic and lasting impact on the native vegetation of some areas. However, over recent years they have created a more noticeable problem in the massive increase in the number of bushflies.

The bushflies have found the cattle dung pat an ideal place in which to live and breed. If the magnitude of this problem is hard to appreciate, do the arithmetic— twenty million cattle depositing twelve dung pats each per day, produces the staggering number of two hundred and forty million per day, nationwide. Four million hectares of ground are covered and so become unproductive in any one year. The pats are not readily broken up and disposed of by the elements, due to the dry climate over much of Australia's major cattle production zones.

Some ten years ago, the authorities were becoming alarmed with the increasing fly and dung pat problem. They were well aware of the role played by the two hundred and fifty or so species of native dung beetles who do a magnificent job in breaking up and disposing of the dung of native animals. However, it was obvious that they had evolved to handle the relatively small droppings of the native creatures, and not the pats of cattle.

For this reason the CSIRO imported and released dung beetles of all sizes and colours from many overseas countries including Turkey, France, Iran, Spain and China. These beetles were more robust types and more suitable to the size of the problem cattle pats. They had the added advantage that, because they came from a wide variety of countries and climates, individual species could be selected to suit the various climatic conditions of the different regions of Australia.

As recently as 1977, we had yet two more species of unwelcome immigrant insects. These arrived in our country having apparently obtained their passage by stowing away in the trouser cuffs of a traveller from America. Quite by accident, he gave a lift to these passengers whilst walking through a lucerne crop. On their arrival here, the spotted alfalfa aphid, and its relative, the blue-green aphid, both easily avoided detection because of their tiny size (two millimetres) and their secure hiding place. The person in whose trouser cuffs they had hitched their ride must have wasted no time in proceeding to wander through an Australian lucerne crop.

So with ample food and in the absence of predators, they bred millions of their kind very quickly. They spread rapidly, assisted by the wind and air currents, to appear virtually everywhere that this valuable stock feed crop was grown in Australia. Their appetite was voracious, and the resulting damage was estimated to have caused losses amounting to fifty million dollars in their first year of freedom.

The authorities acted with urgency. They quickly obtained information regarding controls of these insects in their homeland; these were varieties of fungi and a tiny (two or three millimetre) parasitic wasp. The various forms of the wasp were imported here, tested, and released so as to become the basis for biological control against the troublesome aphids.

Nevertheless, the circumstances surrounding the escape and initial freedom from detection in our country of these two insects serve as a perfect example of the costs involved when pests are introduced. This example highlights the necessity for vigilance and the considerable responsibilities of customs and quarantine officers.

We cannot always expect such rapid successes in controlling troublesome insects as we had in the case of the lucerne aphids; many others remain uncontrolled. Total elimination of unwanted plants and insects is a seemingly unattainable goal, as the overuse of chemicals has proved. The plants and insects simply develop immunity, and seem always to be one jump ahead of the chemical companies' potent concoctions.

Blowflies, for instance, were decimated when DDT was first invented and used against them. However, they became totally immune to it within ten years. Ideally, the use of pesticides and insecticides as control measures will decline, because of their cost, reduced efficiency, and especially because of the growing awareness that they kill multitudes of helpful insects, not the least of which are those imported at great cost as biological control agents.

In fact, once a programme of biological control is started, chemical control must take second place. In addition to the insects already mentioned, we have introduced many more which have proved useful. There are the chrysomela beetles to control St John's wort and the cinnabar moth for the yellow flowered ragwort; the spindly but persistent skeleton weed has succumbed to gall mites and midges expressly imported for its specific control. Many varieties of fungi, rusts, viruses, weevils, borers and blights have been imported and released for particular control of both land and water plants and creatures. Because multitudes of creatures and plants escaped and later prospered in our country, it now seems our unending task to control them by fostering biological control. We have commenced a battle that, although it is hard to see, is raging all the time between many tiny creatures; animal against animal, animal against plant.

It seems the unwanted creatures arrive too frequently in Australia. The light brown fiddleback spider scampered from crates broken whilst being unloaded at a northern sea port. As its venomous bite ranks with the deadly redback and funnelweb, we have no need of it. Similarly, we have no need of the European wasp, well known in its own region for taking the life of man and beast. It is a real nuisance as it swiftly swoops on our food when we eat outdoors.

The Cinnabar Moth.

It has almost prohibited eating in the open throughout much of Europe and we in Australia are not pleased to have this unwelcome guest turn up at our much loved barbecues. It has a dangerous sting, which it can inflict repeatedly; it damages fruit and orchards and is the enemy of the honey bee which it catches and kills on the wing.

Our vigilance must continue, even for the creatures we know, like the cockroach, the world's most successful traveller. It maintains its right to this long held title as it was recently detected in the galleys of overseas jumbo jets. Other creatures repeatedly attempt to gain entry to our country, like the khapra beetle, for they come here in empty ships whose purpose it is to take our grain to world markets. We search out and destroy the dreaded beetles for if they got a hold here they would not only eat our grain in storage, but ruin our hard won reputation as the world's major exporter of clean grain.

Although most insects are tiny creatures, they have a disproportionate effect on our life, particularly when you consider the equipment, manpower and organisation required to deal with them.

Sometimes, when technology fails, control measures take on a novel twist. One local authority who organised war against the Argentine ant menace recruited children. It offered a reward of one hundred dollars to the first child to find a new infestation. They report their findings to a leader wearing an Inspector Anteater costume. Using children in this novel way has merit, as the success of the campaign has proved, for children often frequent dark nooks and crannies, the preferred homesite of the Argentine ant.

Overseas air travellers are also inconvenienced by the constant war waged on insects. As they sit in their high priced seats, the interior of the aircraft is sprayed with insecticide. This causes noses to twitch, others sneeze and cough and some passengers get quite irate. But the insects killed each year by this one method alone are enormous. Local travellers are inconvenienced too as they are restricted from taking fruit from one state to another. The border guards and their road blocks seek to halt the spread of the native Queensland fruit fly, and the accidentally introduced Mediterranean fruit fly.

PLANTS

Before British colonisation, Australia, although a land mass of immense size, was only lightly populated by a nomadic people who were hunters and gatherers. Their existence depended on them wandering in search of food. There were few fruit-bearing trees that were easy to find, or wild vegetables readily available to pick. What the Aborigines ate was totally foreign to the Europeans.

What seemed certain was that for this colony to be self-supporting, cultivated plants of Europe needed to be brought here and established. Fruit trees, vegetables, grains and even grasses for stock were needed if settlers were to eat the foods they were used to. What was available to eat was in meagre quantities, so that it could barely support the relatively small numbers of native inhabitants, and could not be expected to provide for the ever increasing waves of immigrants.

European plants of the main common varieties deemed necessary to sustain the first settlements were hastily dispatched from England, and although some encountered initial setbacks when planted here, others thrived. Australia's climate, seasons and soil types were different from those of Britain, and soon people became aware of the possibilities there were for growing plants from other parts of the world.

A virtual flood of new plants arrived from every corner of the globe; there was probably not one country in the whole world that did not provide us with at least one of their plants. Most were deliberately brought here but many others were unintentionally introduced.

Plants and seeds gathered in foreign countries had the soils of these countries placed about their roots and husks to propagate them or keep them growing, so they would be in a fit state to plant here after their sea voyage. Amongst the soils around imported plants there were the seeds of others, not wanted. To give an idea of just how many varieties of plants came to our shores in these circumstances we might consider the results of experiments made by the noted naturalist Charles Darwin. He took a cup full of mud from the edge of a pond. He spread it out and aired it and in six months five hundred and thirty-seven plants grew from this earth. In another experiment, he took a ball of earth from the foot of a bird killed some three years earlier. From this soil grew eighty-two plants of various kinds.

Most of the varieties of thistles, and indeed many plant species termed 'weeds', came here as a result of being in the soil that surrounded the roots of desirable plants. The unwanted seeds of many species were invariably, although unintentionally, mixed with the food grains, wheat, barley and oats. Everyone was impatient to plant and harvest so as to feed the rapidly expanding settlements. When weeds appeared amongst the growing crops, little heed would have been paid to them; it would cause no surprise as European farmers had learned to live with them amongst their crops.

The weeds and unwanted species sometimes grew better than did the plants deliberately introduced. They seeded, and their seeds were blown great distances by the winds, or were washed away in the soils by floodwaters to be deposited in the silt in new areas.

Birds and other animals carried seeds stuck to their bodies or in the soil on their feet, and deposited them in new parts of the country. These creatures ate the fruit of plants that contained seeds, some of which were undigested and expelled. Many of these took root and flourished; and so the cycle was repeated again and again.

Many exotic plants came here as 'pot plants', imported for their beauty or for no other reason than for curiosity, simply to see if they would grow here. Many did, and more than that—some later carpeted the landscape. Some almost certainly thought a plant's beauty so restricted in the confines of a pot that they planted it out for all to admire.

Some were planted by ordinary folk who were ignorant of what damage may later be caused by their willy-nilly plantings. Others were encouraged to grow by people who should have known better. The king's botanist, Allan Cunningham, in 1817 planted some apple and quince seeds at Mt Binya in southern New South Wales. His expedition leader, John Oxley, wrote that the ceremony was 'more in hope than expectation that the desolate plains will ever be visited by civilised man'.

Foreign plants arrived quite unintentionally, like those in the saddle and feed bags of camels, and in the bed rolls of the Afghans who handled them. They journeyed in outback places, and camel melons, which first grew from the seeds they unknowingly carried, still grow on vines like small pumpkins throughout the areas they trod. It is said that huge purple beans now grow in areas of our inland deserts that the camels and Afghans crossed, just as camel thorn does. Likewise, date palms grow in isolated and lonely places where once these hardy men and their equally hardy animals stopped, ate and disposed of the seeds from the dates. Tourist brochures today entice visitors to the Flinders Ranges in South Australia to view the beautiful wild flowers. The majority of blooms which burst forth each springtime and cover the hills in a sea of colour are not native flowers, but those of wild hops, wild poppy and others that were left behind by the camels and cameleers.

The all too frequent shipwrecks that occurred around our coastline in the early days also provided us with plants from other lands, in what can only be described as the most accidental of circumstances. It was from such circumstances that the first seeds of melilot clover were cast onto the shore of King Island in Bass Strait and escaped from a damaged mattress containing used runners or stems as the inner packing. From this incident a quality stock-fattening grass grew. When later mixed with other grasses, stock feed was produced which has enabled this island to produce prized cattle, and in more recent times, become the winter conditioning pastures for champion racehorses from all over Australia. Ironically 'Kentucky bluegrass', the foundation plant of the American bloodstock industry, entered that country accidentally, as packing for china-ware.

We had a burr arrive from Chile, believed to have first come matted in the tails of horses imported in 1840. It is called the Bathurst burr, and is the small yellowish brown seed pod of a dark green and yellowish bush of murderous spikes.

Left: Camel Melons.

Below: Bathurst Burr.

This bush itself is nasty but the burrs are just as bad, for their spikes have tiny hooks on them, and they cling securely to the wool of sheep (and the hands of shearers!). They cannot be pulled from the fleece or combed out, but must be specially processed with chemicals, thus greatly lowering the value of the wool. Huge sums of money have been spent to eradicate this plant, yet it still persists in most states.

One could be excused for thinking the Bathurst burr may have come from the vast farming areas adjacent to the New South Wales city of that name. This demonstrates that the names given to plants cannot be relied upon to give an accurate description of them, nor an indication as to their origin.

This bush itself is nasty but the burrs are just as bad, for their spikes have tiny hooks on them, and they cling securely to the wool of sheep (and the hands of shearers!). They cannot be pulled from the

have religious overtones: St Barnaby's thistle and St John's wort are but two, which incidentally are most unsaintly as they are considered pests. The apple of Sodom is another pest plant, producing small apple-like fruits. Mother of millions is an apt name and description of a noxious weed in Queensland, such is its free seeding nature.

There is a tree called the tree of heaven; its very name encourages its vigorous and widespread planting yet it is so free-seeding by habit and its roots cause such damage, that it is declared a noxious plant in every state and carries heavy fines for those who plant it. Gentle Annie, or

Right: Patersons Curse.

Below: St. Johns Wart.

fleece or combed out, but must be specially processed with chemicals, thus greatly lowering the value of the wool. Huge sums of money have been spent to eradicate this plant—yet it still persists in most states.

One could be excused for thinking the Bathurst burr may have come from the vast farming areas adjacent to the New South Wales city of that name. This demonstrates that the names given to plants cannot be relied upon to give an accurate description of them, nor an indication as to their origin.

Many of these plants have intriguing names. Some are named after saints, or

innocent weed, is a plant whose name suggests it has a harmless nature, yet its other name is spiny burr grass and it too is a proclaimed noxious weed.

There is no better example of the confusion which surrounds plants because of their multiple names than that which applies to a very widespread plant with purple flowers that is a native of the Mediterranean. It seems to have a different name in each state where it occurs. In Victoria it is called Påterson's curse, indicating its spreading and invasive nature as it smothers more valued pasture grasses. In New South Wales it shares this name or is known as purple weed. South Australia has a kind name for it, Salvation Jane, so called as the saviour of Jane's flock of sheep when drought killed off all other plants less hardy. It is known as Lady Campbell weed in Western Australia, owing to its escape from her garden pot plants which she had gathered in the eastern states.

With so many names in so many localities it was hardly surprising to hear it had attracted another, due to an enterprising truck driver taking a load of this plant to Sydney and selling it in bunches and posies, with the pretty name Riverina bluebell. Eager customers jostled for it. They could have obtained it free of charge, and helped the farmers by doing so, not ten kilometres out of town. This same plant has all of these names, and one can perhaps see how it is regarded in different areas because of them. It has a very close relative that is named viper's bugloss—what went through the mind of the person in giving it this name defies explanation.

Paterson's curse had become so widespread and troublesome in some areas that the authorities felt justified in using biological control measures when all previous control methods failed to have significant effect. However, beekeepers became alarmed at this prospect, for whilst they conceded some control measures were necessary, total eradication of this plant would seriously affect quality

Peppercorn Trees.

honey production. The conflicting arguments for and against control have yet to be resolved.

This plant probably more than any other shows what care needs to be taken before any plant is placed in the category of a 'weed'. A weed can never be more than a plant simply growing out of place. Clover, for example, when growing amongst a crop of vegetables could be called a weed by the market gardener, yet to the grazier, the clover is welcome. With modern technology, the pharmaceutical industry almost daily discovers valuable extracts from previously unwanted plants.

However, many introduced plants are rightfully declared or defined as weeds, or pest plants; no good use has been found for them and, in fact, many grow at serious economic cost for they are hard to get rid of. Some take up space that could otherwise be occupied by more valuable species and thereby reduce potential production of needed plants. Others lower the value and quality of crops by becoming mixed with them during harvest, whilst still others grow so prolifically that they encourage an over-use of chemicals in their control which can have a dramatic effect on wanted plants, animals and insects, as well as getting into our food chain.

So many plants have come to this country by all manner of means that it has been said that we have created a little England about our more inhabited areas. Australia's open spaces, the outback, the inland, the mountains, and the plains and valleys in between, contain so many introduced plants that the entire country could be considered an immense exotic wild garden. So complete has the transportation and establishment of foreign plants been, that when attempting to confirm the origin of any plant it is a more certain bet to assume it is an exotic, rather than a native.

Even the coconut palms which grow about the shorelines of the islands of the Great Barrier Reef, although looking so natural, are not natives but were planted by the Queensland Government in the late 1800s to aid anyone shipwrecked in those waters.

Discerning native and introduced species is not easy. As school children, we collected silkworms from the peppercorn tree as part of nature study classes. During these classes one learnt of the Japanese silkworm which so expertly made the fibre for the cloth from that country. It had been introduced here in the hope that a similar industry might be established. At the same time one learnt that Australia's native silkworm was the caterpillar of the emperor gum moth.

Which of these two silkworms was it that lived amongst the leaves of the peppercorn tree, which was so commonly seen in schoolyards and in the streets of many towns and cities? The peppercorn tree is often the only tree to provide shade on out-back homesteads and to grow surrounded by a virtual sea of sand or red earth so fine nothing else would grow there: surely it must be a native? If not, what would a gum moth be doing in a tree that is not a eucalypt? Or was it that the Japanese silkworm lived in this tree and that the peppercorn tree was not a native, but came from Japan?

Some mysteries are so intriguing that they warrant solving: the peppercorn tree turns out to be a native of South America, and it is the Australian emperor gum moth that has learnt to live and breed in it. The Japanese silkworm, on the other hand, most commonly occurs on the introduced mulberry tree, a native of China (as indeed is the silkworm).

Many plants have reached our shores and have found our countryside much to their liking, and so they have flourished without cultivation. In fact, most introduced plants existing in the wild here came accidentally, for it goes without saying that if financial gain or good use could be had from them, they would most certainly not be wild, but cultivated.

Many plants were brought expressly for cultivation, and although cultivated for a time they outlived their usefulness. Some grew so well here they quickly got out of control, and others had their seeds or fruits spread by natural means so that, although the plant itself was cultivated or controlled, its offspring were able to travel where they liked.

The blackberry was one such plant. There was much joy and celebration when its fruit was first seen growing in Australia but there is no rejoicing now. Initially it was encouraged to grow around the dwellings of the early settlements, and miners always seemed to take it with them. Once they had this plant flourishing they allowed their goats to eat it, thereby ensuring both ample fresh fruit and milk supplies. However, when the miners moved on, often the goats were left to run wild along with the blackberry.

Some blackberry bushes were planted on river banks to stabilise them and to stop them crumbling and being swept away in floods. The willow tree was planted for the same reason. Pieces of the blackberry plant break off during flood and their seeds float down to colonise new areas. Willows spread too. Great trees can grow from broken twigs and branches made into forked sticks and stuck into the soil to be a rest for a fisherman's rod.

There are many types of blackberry, and some nine different species have become widespread. Some patches can be

African Boxthorn.

four metres high and have canes or branches like wire cable that make them impenetrable.

Rabbits find the blackberry a safe haven, sambar deer enjoy their fruit and leaves and find them a good place to rest; they do not seem to be inconvenienced by the sharp hook-like thorns. The fox, the emu and many other birds sometimes exist entirely on their fruits when they ripen in spring. All these creatures, by enjoying the fruit, are major contributors to its wide distribution as they deposit its seeds with their droppings.

The African boxthorn, common in western New South Wales, and the European gorse, which is widespread in Tasmania, are both shrubs that have long, needle-sharp spines, and can grow to heights of two or three metres. They were brought here to be cultivated as hedges for farm properties. However, in most cases they were not carefully maintained, probably because it was not easy to enlist sufficient labour for the uncomfortable work. Property owners soon tired of their upkeep, so simply let them grow wild. Their spread was aided by animals and birds. These two plants, like the blackberry, cover vast amounts of earth that would otherwise grow pasture. Their rambling great bushes now dot the paddocks they were only ever meant to surround.

The prickly pear, and there are many different types, was brought to Australia for a variety of reasons. Some came, it is claimed, with Captain Phillip's First Fleet, although which type is unknown, for this group of cacti occur in many countries. Some are native to the Americas, others to India, Sri Lanka, and other parts of Asia.

There are varieties that arrived in pots, to be admired as ornamentals for their beautiful flowers. Others were grown in gardens for their edible purple pears. Some varieties of prickly pear host a particular parasite, the cochineal insect. The bodies of the females are crushed to extract the well known crimson dye of that name which, since ancient times, has been used to colour cloth. It was used by the English to dye soldiers' uniforms (the Redcoats). It also has other uses such as for food colouring.

Many farmers and graziers thought it a useful plant for containing their stock, and it was vigorously planted for this purpose by hundreds if not thousands of landowners. It made hedges right through central Queensland to the coast, and down to northern New South Wales as well. It was quick growing, hardy and did not need much looking after. It had the added advantage of being able to be chaffed and fed to stock in times of drought; many carted it hundreds of miles for this purpose, then it began to grow on their land.

New settlers were accustomed to hedges. The countryside of England is criss-crossed with them. The hawthorn, which was a favourite hedge plant in England, did not like the warm climate

The flower of the Prickly Pear plant.

but the boxthorn and the cactus did. The hawthorn was restricted to Tasmania and southern Victoria.

Wire for fencing was either prohibitive in cost or not readily available and in any event, posts needed to be cut and sunk into the ground. Posts and rails took labour and there was never enough of that. Plants such as the cactus and the boxthorn must have offered the best alternatives. In many areas there were no trees of the right size or type, and in some places there were no trees at all. What would keep the stock from straying whilst the farmer built such a fence on his land, often a parcel of such size that it was larger than the whole of the district he had emigrated from?

Plants do not keep to rigid well-defined straight lines and so they rapidly spread into the paddocks which they were designed to hedge. The cactus, in particular, grew and spread and eventually almost blanketed the land. It was cut back, chopped, mowed, burned and pulverised, but this only helped to spread it further. Prickly pear became so bad in so many areas that each day the farmers had to dress themselves and their horses in heavy canvas leggings to tackle the cactus.

They could not get the better of it, no matter how hard they tried. It broke them financially and physically too. Thousands

The fruit of the Prickly Pear plant.

left their farms, or what had been farms. By 1900, four million hectares had become infested. For sixty or so years, almost one third of the state of Queensland was overrun by the prickly pear.

The Queensland Government tried hard to encourage selectors to take up blocks that were infested by offering them attractive long leases on condition that they clear the land of prickly pear and keep it clear. There were many takers, but no matter how willing and determined they may have originally been, the cactus still managed to beat most of them. Today it has all but vanished thanks to the insect, cactoblastis.

The pastoralists had also to contend with many other plants which had come here from overseas and, on finding our soils and climate much to their liking, became pest plants. The Noorgoora burr was from the Americas. Like the Bathurst burr, it affects the wool of sheep and has to be scoured from it in the same way, and so lessens the value of the wool. Nature has ensured this plant's survival for it is equipped with two seeds in its brown pod; one strikes the same season as the pod is cast from the plant, whilst the other waits and lies dormant, to strike some seasons later. This habit makes controlling the plant difficult.

The seed pod containing the seeds is like that of most burrs, in that it is armed with spikes which can catch on to almost anything and is readily transported by a great range of creatures. The Noorgoora burr floats and is spread widely by the waters of rivers and streams and especially by the flood waters, however minor, which are a feature of the hot plains country this plant seems to favour.

Many men took on the unenviable job of being full time burr cutters. It is said that some spread the pests to previously uninfested areas, so as to ensure continuity of income.

Farmers whose properties were infested with either of these burrs had working parties to collect them. They gathered the children, the womenfolk and all friends that could be called upon, especially those of neighbouring farms, for if one farm could be entirely cleared, it would prevent the burrs spreading to another and each property could be done in turn.

These were days of scrupulous backbreaking work, for the plants had to be grubbed out, not leaving a trace of the root, and more especially, not a single seed. Inch by inch each paddock was searched, and sheets of hessian were dragged behind for the hooks of the burrs to catch in, just in case some pods had escaped the collectors. Every skerrick of material that was gathered was carefully secured under the hessian cover of the drays. The horses which pulled them even had their hooves wrapped with cloth or hessian so that they too would pick up burrs. Everything collected and used in this meticulous search was heaped and burnt in a great fire, so that nothing could remain of this nuisance to sprout again.

There were thistles too, of every kind, that came in unnoticed amongst other plants. These prickly escapees soon covered many areas and still do.

One was the stemless thistle from the Mediterranean that grew, not as an upright plant as most thistles do, but as a flat circular plant the size of a dinner

Left: Prickly Pear infestation.

Below: Stemless Thistle.

plate. Individual specimens are most attractive and unusually interesting but one would not like paddocks full of them.

The saffron thistle produces a lovely flower, but it has menacing thistle spikes. It grows in very dense stands, and today it still occurs throughout much of the dry plains grazing areas. It has become so impenetrable on some properties that road grading machines have to smash and flatten it down before men and dogs are able to move amongst it to muster sheep.

Many thistles produce pretty flowers, among them the golden thistle and the

Scotch Thistle.

abundant spear or black thistle whose purple flower head is commonly confused with the Scotch thistle.

The thistle family must certainly be the most widespread of all our introduced plants. There seems to be at least one or more varieties that are well suited to each and every type of terrain. Some are small and delicate, almost unobtrusive, like the milkweed that grows in suburban gardens. This plant, incidentally, is credited with having brought the Pacific wanderer butterfly to our country. Its habit has been to follow this plant around the world. It is said to have island hopped from country to country around the globe from its native America.

Other thistles are by their very size obtrusive and almost threatening; the massive artichoke thistle is one of these. It is a colossus amongst thistles, a single plant can cover an area three to four metres square. It is as tall as a man and its outer edges are armed with rows of extremely sharp spikes.

Nature has so equipped the seeds of many of these plants that their survival and spread was almost guaranteed. Many seeds of thistle species are of 'parachute design' (like those of the dandelion), being easily caught by late summer winds and taken to far off places. At such times of the year, in areas of heavy infestation, great clouds of seeds can be seen drifting on air currents and floating across the landscape. They spread vast distances this way and finally come to rest against logs, rocks, fences and buildings, but more especially in ploughed ground. Most of these plants are essentially 'plants of cultivation' and their seeds are not designed to penetrate hard-packed virgin soil; instead they must rely on broken ground to enable their future growth.

In the early days, there were innumerable teams of stout-bodied horses, driven by men of even stouter hearts, who broke this land in with the plough at a considerable pace, and throughout a huge area. By their very efforts they unwittingly gave thistles and other weeds of cultivation the opportunities to grow, seed and thrive again, as they had done in Europe. Such plants, had long been a nuisance in the cultivated lands of Europe, where time was allotted each year for their cutting.

Hand cutting was done here too, although never to the same extent as commonly occurred on the more labour intensive farms of Europe. Australian farms were generally of a much greater size, and early on they did not produce sufficient income to employ workers to prevent nuisance plants from growing and spreading.

The thistles, burrs and other unwanted plants were greatly assisted in their spread and colonisation of new areas by sheep. Sheep numbers rapidly increased from the arrival of the First Fleet to total

Pacific Wanderer Butterfly.

an estimated one hundred million only a hundred years later.

Sheep took the seeds of nuisance plants with them. There is no better medium than the wool of sheep for seeds, prickles and the spines of plants to catch on. Sheep also eat such plants, swallow their seeds and some time later expel them, allowing the seed to strike and grow anew.

There was a great overland movement of sheep that occurred in this hundred year period (1788–1888), for there were a hundred million stomachs to fill. Native plants and grasses had not evolved to be so closely cropped by so many mouths, nor to be trodden on by four hundred million hard cloven hooves. Native creatures are soft footed, and do not bite growth off short, nor so completely. Sheep had to be constantly moved to obtain new feed. They were moved in huge numbers back and forth from one area to another by many graziers, due to drought, lack of feed or for the movement of breeding stock, and also to avail themselves of any price advantage that could be had from shifting them from one area to another.

Many farmers on the land today can either recall themselves, or relate stories from their families regarding the first arrival of burry and prickly sheep to their district.

This uncontrolled grazing came to a rapid halt in the drought of 1895–1902; it was the worst of many such droughts that are a feature of Australia. Sheep were pulled back from country they had eaten out. Rabbits were at their worst at this time and they contributed significantly towards eating the country bare. Sheep numbers dropped drastically to almost half. The native vegetation in many areas has still not recovered, and most probably will not see sheep again. Nevertheless the plants the sheep originally carried in with them stayed on, and are now all too commonly seen.

Many unwanted plants that now grow wild are often referred to as garden escapees. As the homesteaders and free settlers began to move inland from the original coastal settlements, they took with them seeds and seedlings of vegetables, grains and other plants. The womenfolk, in particular, took with them cuttings, slips and seeds of foreign garden plants. What better way to feel at home here, than to have flowers that were the same as they had known in England?

To European eyes, the vegetation of this new country was very often seen to be monotonous, drab and of indistinct colouration. Could some semblance of civilisation be created by planting exotic blooms?

As visitors passed through these lonely outstations, they were given not only hospitality, but plants, cuttings and seeds as well to take with them, so they too may have an exotic garden. It is a very old custom for people to give plants to others who may have admired them growing, or who felt their own garden might be improved by their transplanting, just as Lady Campbell did, and Mrs Paterson too, and it is still a common practice.

There is no doubt that there was considerable traffic in such plants in the

Artichoke Thistle.

early days, such is their wide distribution now. Many of them grew so well, they seeded and were spread by wind, weather, animals and birds to new areas. Once there, they grew wild. The tangled vine of the lantana had such beginnings, as did the wild rose or sweet briar, whose pretty pink and white blooms are the forebear of all modern garden roses.

The Great Dividing Range in south-east Australia consists of rows of steep hills, very often with steep valleys in between. Some parts are so rugged and remote that one can walk for days and come across little valleys very few other people would have passed through. One I know is surrounded by massive, sheer, sandstone bluffs. Great trees of enormous girth grow on the valley sides. The floor has a fast-flowing stream that twists and turns through open park-like glens. It comes from a waterfall that cascades fifty metres down from yet another range above.

It was spring when I was there and the whole valley was ablaze with yellow wild flowers; there seemed hardly space enough for grass to grow, the flowers were so thick. Alas, the wildflowers were not native ones, but those of St John's wort. One wonders if there is anywhere in Australia that foreign plants have not invaded.

After long and sometimes difficult walks one can come upon old cabins and musterers' huts in the mountains, both on the mainland and in Tasmania. They were built entirely of timber except for a rock fireplace. Their owners' stay in them was brief, hardship forced them out, and they have remained deserted for perhaps fifty or a hundred years.

The weather and the elements have taken toll of them and they are falling down and decaying at a rapid rate.

Daffodils.

Perhaps in another fifty or one hundred years there may be no visible signs of them apart from the daffodils whose bulbs were planted about them by those hardy souls who tried to make a go of it in such isolated locations. The pioneers came and went, but the pretty flowers still come up each year to herald spring. Future generations of bushwalkers will doubtless venture into such places, and be mystified by these patches of daffodils.

Plants were doubtless introduced into our waterways when people disposed of their aquarium fish, most probably thinking this to be a kindly and humane act. Not only did wild populations of fish result, but wild populations of water plants flourished too, for they were tipped in along with the fish.

The Canadian pond weed is one, alligator weed and salvinia are others; and they are all causing problems as they are capable of spreading in a most alarming way. However, it is the water hyacinth from South America that is of most concern, for it has the potential, if unchecked, to spread across waterways just as the prickly pear spread over land.

The water hyacinth is a native of Venezuela, and is a flat, wrinkly-leaved lily plant. It is equipped with bladder-like sections which enable it to float, and it has a most attractive mauve flower which no doubt was the reason for its popularity.

This water plant has a certain innocence when contained in tanks or ornamental ponds which belies its true wild habit. It is truly invasive by nature and rapidly takes over relatively shallow waterways and irrigation channels; its density of growth blocks pumps, turbines and any other mechanical water control device. It is equally at home in deep waters of ten metres or more—in some countries it has spread and blocked major rivers completely, so that large ocean-going ships are denied access to up-river wharves.

In addition to the blocking habit of the water hyacinth, its growth pattern causes another problem. The vigorous new growth occupies the surface water layer and forces the mature and ageing leaves underwater, causing them to quickly decompose. This results in an ever increasing build up of slimy rotting material which gives off foul odours and makes the water putrid and inky black. It affects the water quality to such a degree that it is totally unfit to drink for both humans and animals.

These introduced water plants occur in

Left: Canadian Pondweed.

Water Hyacinth.

many localities in eastern Australia, and large sums of money are constantly being spent on their control. The authorities are particularly concerned with the water hyacinth, for it invades the watercourses of the flat plains country of northern New South Wales. The flooding nature of the streams in which it grows may cause it to gain entry to the vast network of irrigation channels as well as major river systems, such as the Murray, from which drinking water is drawn for large towns and cities.

All these water plants now grow in the wild here, largely as a result of accidental or careless actions. They are a serious problem, one that will require ongoing control if they are to be contained.

Many other introduced plants are poisonous to both humans and animals. For example, the ragwort has caused the milk from dairy cows to be unfit to drink. Capeweed causes irritation to the tongues of cattle who lick their hides to gain some relief. Hair balls can then cause cattle to choke. There are a great many other plants that cause a wide variety of such ills and maladies, and none are of such beauty that it outweighs their danger in this their new country.

However, not all plants that were brought here and now live in what can be considered a wild state are classed as problem plants. The authorities have found that good use can be made of the marram grass and the African boneseed, both African desert plants, and now widely planted to stabilise the eroding sand dunes of many coastal beaches.

Summary of Introductions

Name	Purpose	Original Native Range	Main Concentrations in Australia
Animals			
Blackbuck Antelope *Antilope cervicapra*	Sport	India	WA
Chital/Axis Deer *Axis axis*	Sport	S/E Asia	Qld private property
Fallow Deer *Dama dama*	Sport	Central and Southern Europe	All states except NT and WA
Hog Deer *Axis pronicus*	Sport	India	Vic east coast
Red Deer *Cervus Elephus*	Sport	Eurasia	Qld, NSW, WA, Vic
Rusa Deer *Cervus timorenis*	Sport	S/E/ Asia	Qld, NSW, NT
Sambar Deer *Cervus unicolour*	Sport	S/E/ Asia	Eastern Vic, Coburg Pen NT
Cane Toad *Bufo marinus*	Cane beetle control 1935	South America	Qld, Nth NSW coast
Fox *Vulpes vulpes*	Sport	Europe	Aust wide, not Tas
Hare *Lepus capensis*	Sport	Eurasia/Africa	Aust wide except tropics
House Mouse *Mus musculus*	Accidental	Europe	Aust wide
Rat (Black) *Rattus rattus*	Accidental	S/E Asia	Aust wide
Rat (Brown) *Rattus norvegicus*	Accidental	Eurasia	Aust wide
Rabbit *Oryctolagus cuniculus*	Sport	Eurasia	Aust wide except tropics
Birds			
Blackbird *Turdus merula*	Aesthetics	Europe	NSW, Vic, SA
Bulbul (Red-whiskered) *Pycnonotus jocosus*	Aesthetics	Asia, Africa	Vic, NSW
Cattle Egret *Ardeola ibis*	1930 Cattle tick control	Asia, Africa	Tropical Aust
English Skylark *Alauda avensis*	Aesthetics	Europe	Southern Aust
Goldfinch *Carduelis carduelis*	Aesthetics	Eurasia	Southern Aust
Greenfinch *Carduelis chloris*	Aesthetics	Europe	Tas, SA, Vic, NSW
Hedge Sparrow *Passer montanus*	Aesthetics	Europe	Vic, NSW
Indian Peafowl *Pavo cristatus*	Aesthetics	India	WA
Indian Mynah *Acridotheres tristis*	Asthetics	S/E Asia	Vic, SA, NSW, Qld
Mallard Duck *Anus platyrhynchos*	Food	Europe	Most states
Ostrich *Struthio camelus*	Feather industry	Africa	SA
Partridge (Chukar) *Perdix* sp	Sport	Eurasia	NSW
Pheasant *Phasianus colchicus*	Sport	Eurasia	King Island Tas, WA
Quail (California) *Lophortyx californicus*	Sport	USA	King Island Tas
Song Thrush *Turdus philomelos*	Aesthetics	Europe	Vic
Sparrow (House) *Passer domesticus*	Aesthetics	Europe	Aust wide except NT and WA
Starling *Sturnus vulgaris*	Aesthetics	Europe	Aust wide except NT and WA
Turtle Doves *Streptopelia* sp	Aesthetics	Southern Asia	Southern Aust, Qld
White Swan *Cygnus olar*	Aesthetics	Europe	WA, Tas

Name	Purpose	Original Native Range	Main Concentrations in Australia
Fish			
Aquarium Fish	Accidental	Asia	Various locals, most states
Carp *Cyprinus carpio*	Food fish in ponds, tanks	Eurasia	South mainland Aust
Coarse Fish: Tench *Tinca tinca*	Food/sport	Europe	All states except WA and NT
Roach *Rutilus rutilus*	Food/sport	Europe	S/E/States and Qld
Dace *Leuciscus leuciscus*	Food/sport	Europe	Tas
European Perch *Perca fluviatilis*	Sport	Europe	All states except NT
Redfin	Food/sport	Eurasia	NT
Goldfish *Carassius auvatus*	Accidental	Eurasia	All states except NT
Mosquito Fish/Gambusia *Gambusia affinis*	1930s mosquito control	Americas/Middle East	Vic, Qld, NSW, Tas, SA, NT
Pacific Oyster *Ostreidae* sp	1902 food industry	Japan	Tas
Salmon: Atlantic *Salmo salar*	1906 sport	North Atlantic	NSW, landlocked
Salmon: Quinnat *Oncorhynchus tshawytscha*	1930 sport	America, Nth Pacific	Western Vic, landlocked
Trout: Brown *Salma trutta*	1860 sport	Europe	All states except NT
Trout: Eastern Brook *Salvalinus fontinalis*	1900 sport	USA	Tas, NSW
Trout: Rainbow *Salmo gairdneri*	1860 Sport	USA	All states except NT

Special notes re: summary

1. Most deliberate introductions were made by Acclimatization Societies, in various states, during the 1860's.
2. Other deliberate introductions were made by many private individuals and groups, to many areas, both before and after the 1860's.
3. Therefore, whilst every attempt was made to include all those creatures (obviously not all plants and insects due to the high numbers), that presently occur in the wild of Australia; this list cannot be entirely completed for there always exists the possibility of other exotics being in the wild.
4. This summary also does not include those that were deliberately introduced that (a) failed to be released, or (b) and/or failed to establish themselves when seet free for a variety of reasons.
5. This summary also does not include the considerable number and variety of plants and insects in particular, that were accidentally introduced, (due to the complexity).
6. Re Feral Animals, as they are all 'once domesticated' species; scientific naming and release points was not considered appropriate.

   Most are generally found Australia-wide, in scattered locations; having escaped or been abandoned since settlement.

Wild Plants

Common name	Latin or Scientific Name
African Boneseed	*Chrysanthemoides monilifera*
African Boxthorn	*Lyciumferocissimum*
Alligator Weed	*Alternanthera philoxeroides*
Angels Trumpet	*Brugmansia* x *candida*
Apple of Sodom	*Solanum sodomeum*
Artichoke Thistle	*Cynara carduneulus*
Arum Lily	*Zanthedeschia aethiopica*
Bathurst Burr	*Xanthium spinosum*
Blackberry	*Rubus fruticosus vulgaris* (various)
Black Thistle	*Cirsium vulgare*
Camel Melon	*Colocynthis citrullus*
Camel Thorn	*Alhagi pseudalhagi*
Canadian Pondweed	*Elodea canadensis*
Capeweed	*Cryptostemma calendula*
Castor Oil Plant	*Rieinus communis*
Coconut Palm	*Cocos nucifera*
Coral Bush	*Jatropha podagrica*
Daffodil	*Narcissus pseudo narcissus*
Dandelion	*Taraxacum officinale*
Date Palm	*Phoenix dactylifera*
European Gorse	*Ulex europaeus*
Gentle Annie	*Cenchrus longis pinus*
Golden Dewdrop	*Duranta* sp.
Golden Thistle	*Scolymus hispanicus*
Hawthorn	*Crataegus* sp.
Hemlock	*Conium maculatum*
Lantana	*Lantana camara*
Marram Grass	*Ammophila arenaria*
Melilot Clover	*Melilotus* sp.
Milk Weed	*Sonchus oleraceus*
Mother of Millions	*Bryophyllum* sp.
Mulberry Tree	*Morus alba*
Naked Lady	*Euphorbia tirucalli*
Noorgoora Burr	*Xanthium pungens*
Oleander	*Nerium oleander*
Paterson's Curse	*Echium plantagineum*
Peppercorn Tree	*Schinus* sp. (Molle)
Prickly Pear	*Opuntia inermis* and *stricta*
Privet	*Ligustrum* sp.
Ragwort	*Senecio jacobaea*
Saffron Thistle	*Carthamus lanatus*
Salvinia	*Salvinia molesta*
Scotch Thistle	*Onopordum acanthium*
Silverleaf Nightshade	*Solanum elaeagnifolium*
St Barnaby's Thistle	*Centaurea solstitialis*
St Johns Wort	*Hypericum perforatum*
Stemless Thistle	*Onopordum acaulon*
Tree of Heaven	*Ailanthus altissima*
Water Hyacinth	*Eichhornia crassipes*
Wild Hop	*Rumex vesicarius*
Wild Poppy	*Papaver lybridium*
Wild Rose	*Rosa rubiginosa*

Introduced Insects

Common Name	Latin or Scientific Name
Alfalfa Aphids, spotted blue green	*Theriophis maculata* Blue Green: *Acryphosphoron kondoi*
Aphids (various)	*Aphididae* sp.
Argentine Ant	*Iridomyrmex humilis*
Bed Bugs	*Cimex lectularius*
Blights	Various
Bots (Cattle and Sheep)	*Destridae* and *Gastro philidae*
Buffalo Fly	*Simuliidae*
Cactoblastis Moth	*Cactoblastis cactorum*
Chrysomela Beetles	*Chrysomela gemellata, hyperic*
Cinnibar Moth	*Hypocrita jacobaeae*
Clothes Moths	*Tineidae* sp.
Cochineal Insect	*Chelinidea tabulata*
Cockroaches	European: *Blattella germanica* US: *Periplanta americana* Asian: *Blatta orientalis*
Codling Moth	*Carpocaspa pomonella*
Dung Beetles	*Scarabaeinae* sp.
Earwig	*Forficula auricularia*
European Wasp	*Paravespula germanica*
Fiddleback Spider	*Loxosceles refuscens*
Fleas (various)	*Siphonaptera* sp.
Fungi (various)	Various
Gall Mites	Various
Garden Snails	*Helix aspersa*
Giant African Snail	*Achatina fulica*
Grain Weevils	*Sitophilus granarius*
Harlequin Bug	*Dindymus vericolor*
Honey Bee	*Apis mellifera*
House Fly	*Musca domestica*
Indian Termite	*Cryptotermes brevis* and *primus*
Japanese Silkworm	*Bombyx mori*
Khapra Beetle	*Trogoderma granarium*
Lice (various)	*Anoplura* sp.
Mediterranean Fruit Fly	*Ceratatis capitata*
Midges (various)	*Diptera* sp.
Mites (various)	*Acari* sp.
Mole Cricket	*Gryllotalpa africana*
Myxomatosis Virus	Virus
Parasitic Wasp	*Opius* sp.
Potato Moth	*Gelechiidae* sp.
Rabbit Flea	*Spilopsyllus cuniculi*
Rusts (various)	Various
Sheep Blowfly	*Lucilia cuprina*
Silverfish	*Lepisma saccharina*
Slater/Wood Louse	*Isopods* sp.
Slugs (various)	*Arion hortensis*
Spargana Tapeworm	*Spirometra erinacei*
Stable Fly	*Stomoxys calcitrans*
Steam Borer	*Epiblema strenuana*
Ticks (various)	*Ixodidae/Argasidae*
White Snail	*Gastropoda* sp.
Yellow Snail	*Gastropoda* sp.

INDEX

Aboriginal food 4, 104
acclimatization societies 5, 11
Afghan camel drivers 65, 105
African boneseed 114
African Boxthorn 108-9
African snail 116
Ailanthus trees 119-20
alligator weed 113
Alpine Dingo 72, 76
Alsatian dogs 75
aphids 115, 122
apple trees 105
Apple of Sodom 106
aquarium fish 102-3
archer fish 94
Argentine ant 116
artichoke thistle 111
artificial rearing 9
Asian black rat 43
Asian wild carp 102
Atlantic salmon 95, 97
Australian Ground Thrush 77

bandicoots 8
banteng cattle 67
barramundi 94
Bathurst burr 58, 105-6, 110
Batman, John 4
bedbugs 115
beehives 42, 119
see also European Honey bees
beekeepers 107
bellbirds 77
bilbies 8
Bill carts 69
biological control 9, 122-3
    of Paterson's Curse 107
    of prickly pear 110, 120-1
    of rabbits 121
birds
    as pollinators and seed spreaders 7-8, 104-5, 119
'Black Death' 43
black duck 90-1
black swan 77, 86
black thistle 111
blackberry 108
blackbird 30, 80-1
blackbuck antelope 17, 34-5
blowflies 118-19
blue green aphid 122
Bogong High Plains 46
bots 117
Brahman cattle 118
Brazilian cacti 120
breeding programmes 9
British farming practices 6, 112
bronzewing pigeons 89
brook trout 97
brown fiddleback spider 123
brown trout 50, 94-6
brumbies 23-4, 46-7
see also mustangs
Brumby Plain 46
bubonic plague 43
bucks 13
buffalo flies 66
bulbul 85
Burke & Wills 5, 48
burr cutting 110
bush flies 118, 121
bush turkeys 89
see also feral turkeys
bustards 8

cabbage moths 62, 116
cacti 108-9
cactoblastis 110
California quail 89-90
calves 13
camel melons 56, 105
camel thorn 105
camels 48, 65, 105
Canadian pond weed 102, 113
canaries 84
cane toad 6, 22, 41-2
capeweed 114
carp 100-2
cashmere 70
cats
see feral cats
cattle
    dung 121-2
    humped breeds 67
    ticks 67, 88, 117-18
cattle egret 88, 118
chevron 70
chital deer 33-4
chooks 93
chrysomela beetles 122
Chuckar partridge 89-90
cinnabar moth 63, 122
clothes moths 115-16
cloven hooves 7, 112
clover 105, 107
coarse fish 99-100
Cochineal Scale insect 120
cockateils 8
cockatoos 7, 77
cockroaches 115-17, 123
coconut palms 107
cod 94
codling moth 61, 115-16
commercial eradication 9
commercial hatcheries 9
Cook, James 4
corellas 8
cows 13
crocodiles 9
crows 8
crucian carp 102
CSIRO 122
Cunningham, Alan 105
customs services 10

dace 99-100
daffodils 55, 113
Dampier, William 4
dandelions 55
Dargo 46
Darwin, Charles 104
date palms 105
DDT 8, 122
Dead Horse Gap 46
deer 5, 11-16, 34
deer wallows 12
dingo fence 73, 74-5
dingoes 8, 27, 73-6
    Aboriginal relationship with 73-4
    crossbreeding with feral dogs 75
    population growth 74
does 13
dogs
see feral dogs
donkeys 47-8
dung beetles 42, 122

earwig 116
East Gippsland 71
Eastern brook trout 97
Emperor gum moth 64, 108, 119
emus 9, 11, 77, 92, 108
English Skylark 82-3
eradication 9
European brown rat 43
European Carp 50
European goldfinch 84
European gorse 108
European greenfinch 85
European Honey bee 119
see also beehives
European house mouse 43
European perch 98-9
European Sheep Greenbottle fly 118-19
European Wasp 123

fallow deer 12-13, 18
fawns 13
fencing 40, 65
feral animals
    how they spread 45-6
feral cats 6, 9, 40, 70-1
feral dogs 6, 28, 71-2
feral domestic fowls 93
feral goats 26, 69-70
feral pigeons 50, 91-2
feral pigs 9, 25, 67-9, 117
feral turkeys 93
see also bush turkeys
finches 7
fish imports methods of transport 95
flame robin 77
fleas 115, 117
flies 118-119
Flinders Ranges 105
flowered ragwort 63, 122
foot and mouth disease 66
fox 5-6, 9, 20, 35-6, 108
foxskins 9, 35
fruit fly 61, 123
funnelweb spiders 123

galahs 8, 77
gall mites 123
gambusia 103
garden escapees 112
Gentle Annie 106
German shepherd dogs 75
giant clams 9
goannas 8
Goat Island 93
goatmeat 70
goats
see feral goats
gold discoveries 4, 45
golden thistle 111
goldfish 102
grasses
    South American 10
ground lark 82-3
guppy 102

hares 40-1
harlequin bug 116
harriers 8
hawks 8
hedge sparrow 79
helicopter mustering 66
heliothus moth 8
hind 13
hog deer 15-16
honey 119
honey production 107
honeyeaters 7
house sparrow 78

Indian mynah 83-4
Indian peafowl 87
Indian spotted dove 86-7
Indian termite 116
Innocent weed 106
irrigation channels 65

Japanese silkworm 107-8, 119-20

Kalgoorlie 65
kangaroos 4, 8-9, 11
'Kentucky bluegrass' 105
khapra beetles 123
Kimberleys 10, 48, 88
King Island 90, 105
kites 8
koalas 9
kookaburra 77
Kosciusko Ranges 46

Lady Campbell weed 106, 112
Lake Eyre 69

lantana 60, 112
leopard fish 102
lice 115
locusts 8
Longreach 69
'Longreach Lamb' 69
lungfish 94
lyrebird 77

macadamia nuts 4
magpie geese 66
magpies 77
malaria 103
Mallard duck 90-1
marram grass 114
McNamara, Dame Jean 39
mealy bugs 64
Mediterranean fruit fly 61, 123
melilot clover 105
Melville Island 66
mice 8, 43
see also native mice
midges 123
milkweed 111
mohair 26, 69, 70
mole cricket 116
monocultures 8
Mort, Thomas 74
mosquito fish 103
mosquitoes 103, 121
mountain dingo
see Alpine Dingo
Mt Binya 105
mulberry trees 108, 119-20
mules 48
Murray cod 94, 101
mustangs in USA 9
see also brumbies
mute swan 85-6
mynah 83-4

native blowflies 118
native cats 8
native ducks 89, 90-1
native flora
    impact of grazing 7-9, 112
    impact of settlement 7-9
native forests 7
native mice 8, 43
see also mice
native rats 8, 43
see also rats
native species
    artificial rearing 9
Native Wild Dog Foundation 76
Nile perch 10
Norgoora burr 110
Northwest Island 93

Omeo 46
Ord River Valley 10
ostriches 92
Overland Telegraph 65
owls 8
Oxley, John 105

Pacific oyster 103
Pacific Wanderer butterfly 111
'palmated' antlers 13
paradise fish 102
parasitic wasp
    to control aphid 122
parrots 7, 77
Paterson's Curse 106-7, 112
Paterson, Banjo 46
Pathan camel drivers 65
peacocks 87
peppercorn tree 64, 107-8
pest control 116
pharmaceutical industry 107
Phillip, Arthur 4
pigeons
see feral pigeons
pigs
see feral pigs
pipit 82-3
plants of cultivation 111-12
poisoning 28
    1080 39-40
population control 8
Port Sorrell 103
possums 8
pot plants 105
potato moth 116
prickly pear 52-3, 108-110, 113
    biological control 110, 120-1
purple beans 105
purple weed 106

quail 89
quarantine services 10
Queensland fruit fly 123
quince trees 105
Quinnat salmon 98

rabbit flea 121
rabbit warren 22
rabbits 5-6, 21, 37-40, 74, 108, 112
    breeding 38-9
    fencing 40, 65
    impact on environment 37-8
    myxomatosis 39, 121
    why they are a pest 38
ragwort 114
rainbow trout 95-6
rats 8, 43-4
see also native rats
red deer 11-12, 18
red-whiskered bulbul 85
redback spiders 123
redfin 98-9
ringneck pheasant 31, 88-9
'risk goods' 10
river siltation 7
Riverina Bluebell 106
roach 99-100
rosellas 77
Rottnest Island 89
Royal Park, Melbourne 5
ruminants 33
rusa deer 16, 33

saffron thistle 110-11
salmon 95, 101
Salvation Jane 106
salvinia 113
sambar deer 14-15, 19, 108
Sassafras 46
Scotch thistles 57, 111
seeds
    spread of 7-8, 104-5, 119
Senegal turtle dove 86-7
seri culture 120
settlement growth 4-5
settlers
    re-creation of 'home' 5
sheep 36, 74, 112
    Flystrike 118-19
Silkworm moths 120
silkworms 107, 119-20
silverfish 115-16
singing bushlark 82
skeleton weed 123
slater 116
slugs 116
snails 82, 116
snakes 8
Snowgums 46
soil erosion 7
song thrush 30, 81-2
songbirds 80-3
spangled perch 94
Sparganosis 117
sparrow 78-9
spear thistle 111
spiny burr grass 106
spotted alfalfa aphid 122
St Barnaby's thistle 106
St John's wort 57, 106, 113, 122

stable fly 117
star thistles 59
starling 29, 79-80
steelhead 96
stemless thistle 58, 110
stickfast fleas 8
sweet briar 112
swordtail 102
Sydney rock oyster 103

tapeworms 117
tench 99-100
thistles 110-112
'thrushes anvil' 82
ticks
    cats 117
    cattle 67, 88, 117-18
    dogs 117
    poultry 117
tigers 14
Timor ponies 46
Trans Continental railway 65
Trap Yard Hill 46
Tree of heaven 106
trout 5, 94-7, 101
turkeys
see bush turkeys
    feral turkeys

venison 13
Victorian Zoological Society 5
vine hawk moth 60
vine moth 63
Viper's Bugloss 107

wallabies 8
warrigals 8
water buffalo 24, 66-7
water hyacinth 54, 102, 113-14
wedgetailed eagles 9
weeds 107
weevils 115
white cockatoos 8, 77
white swan 85-6
wild goats
see feral goats
wild hops 105
wild horses
see brumbies
    mustangs
wild pigs
see feral pigs
wild poppy 105
wild rose 112
willow tree 108
willy wagtail 77
wombats 8
wool transport
    camels 65
    donkeys 47
Woolybutts 46

yellowbelly 94

Zebu cattle 67, 117-18